The World's Most Haunted Hospitals

True-Life Paranormal Encounters in Asylums,
Hospitals, and Institutions

THE

WORLD'S MOST
HAUNTED HOSPITALS

Richard Estep

THE WORLD'S MOST HAUNTED HOSPITALS
TYPESET BY KRISTIN GOBLE
Printed in the U.S.A.
Front cover images: Surgery room photo by kre_geg/iStock; Hospital ruins photo by Sean Pavone/iStock; Wheelchair photo by stuart renneberg/iStock; Back cover image by Patrick Foto/shutterstock

To order this title, please call toll-free 1-800-CAREER-1 (NJ and Canada: 201-848-0310) to order using VISA or MasterCard, or for further information on books from Career Press.

The Career Press, Inc.
12 Parish Drive
Wayne, NJ 07470
www.careerpress.com
www.newpagebooks.com

Library of Congress Cataloging-in-Publication Data
Names: Estep, Richard, 1973-
Title: The world's most haunted hospitals : true-life paranormal encounters
    in asylums, hospitals, and institutions / by Richard Estep.
Description: Wayne : Career Press, Inc., 2016. | Includes bibliographical
    references and index.
Identifiers: LCCN 2015037787| ISBN 9781632650269 | ISBN 9781632659729 (ebook)
Subjects: LCSH: Haunted hospitals. | Asylums--Miscellanea.
Classification: LCC BF1474.4 .E88 2016 | DDC 133.1/22--dc23 LC record available at http://lccn.loc.gov/2015037787

This book is dedicated to those who do not accept themselves as being in a dead end, but are able to change their path regardless of age, experience, and background. These are the people who challenge themselves, renew, relearn, and take the rest of us into new and wonderful places with them. The author should recognize himself as one of these exceptional people.

ACKNOWLEDGMENTS

If you are thinking that the dedication of this book was a little self-important, particularly the phrase "the author should recognize himself as one of these exceptional people," you should thank Ade Barwick. Ade won my charity auction by donating a significant amount of money to *The Teenage Cancer Trust* (*www.teenagecancertrust.org*) in exchange for writing the dedication himself (and embarrassing the author into the bargain!).

This book would not have been possible without the time, passion, and assistance of the many individuals who contributed to its writing, generously sharing their stories of haunted healthcare facilities from around the world. All credit goes to them, and any errors made are the responsibility of the author.

- Dr. Alison Leary
- Annie Lindsay at the National Health Service
- Kelvin Tan of 360 Snapshots and Amber Moose, photographers extraordinaire, and the kind uploaders to Wikimedia Commons, for brightening up the book
- Hung of *www.Hungzai.com* for graciously sharing stories of Changi
- Marcus Lindsey and Clare Benavides of Paranormal EXP

- Jason and Angela Arnold of Contact Paranormal
- Darren from Ghost Research International
- Paranormal investigator Joe Mendoza
- Rob Calzada and Golden Crescent Paranormal
- The Old Yoakum Hospital Group
- Media maestro Noel Boyd and the crew from "Ghost Files Singapore"
- Author Robin Saikia
- Hazel Bishop and the West Houston Paranormal Society
- Russell Rush and his "Haunted Tour" team
- Author Marty Young
- Susan Wallner of Final Dimension Paranormal
- Matthew Didier and John Savoie at PsiCan
- Jim "Harry the Horse" Dale
- Urban explorers Robert Joe and Brian J. Cano
- Mike Sculley
- Andy Laird of the Rhode Island Paranormal Research Society
- Laura Giuliano from the Para-Boston Team
- Bloggers Shuko K. Tamao ("Reversed View of Massachusetts") and J.W. Ocker ("Odd Things I've Seen")
- Kimm and Cami Andersen, Misty Grimstead, and Dusty Kingston of Asylum 49
- Barry Fitzgerald of "Ghost Hunters International"
- Marcelle Hanauer and Chuck Thornton of St. Albans
- Chris Balassone of Tri-State Paranormal
- Michael Cardinuto of L.I.P.I.
- Zak Bagans, Nick Groff, and Aaron Goodwin
- Author George Dudding
- Laura Estep, Jason and Linda Fellon, Sean Rice, Mike and Caren Kraft, Charlie Stiffler, Catlyn Keenan, Kira and Seth Woodmansee, and the investigators from BCPRS

CONTENTS

FOREWORD

Some people may ask the question: "Why would an old hospital be haunted?" Well, I ask: "Why wouldn't it be?" As someone who has been in the medical field for more than 20 years, which includes being a Licensed Practical Nurse working on a Med/Surg floor and my current position working as a paramedic in the field, I can tell you that it makes a lot of sense. Look at all the trauma that comes into the hospitals, for instance, the sudden deaths and the near-death experiences (NDEs). That's not even including the specialty hospitals such as the psychiatric hospitals and tuberculosis hospitals. There are so many old hospitals around this country that have been deemed haunted; for instance, Old South Pittsburg Hospital, Rolling Hills Asylum, St. Albans (my favorite), and that is just to name a very few.

There is a lot of energy that is left over from when these hospitals were active, where people have passed away. Energy never dissipates, so it is possible that the energy is still within the walls and is released at certain times. You can also think of it as souls who feel that they are stuck in these buildings and don't know how to move on. No matter which side you lean toward, you have to admit hospitals are good places to start looking for paranormal activity. Some of the hospitals around the world are conducting a type of paranormal research. These hospitals are researching NDEs by putting certain words up near the ceiling, in places where nobody on the floor can see them. If they have a patient that "codes" (dies) and comes back, the patient is asked whether they experienced an NDE. You have to admit that is pretty cool for modern medical science to be looking into the paranormal!

There are also a number of medical conditions that can explain certain paranormal experiences. For instance, there are people who will smell something specific and believe that it is a loved one letting them know that they are there. It has actually been proven that if it is just one single person in a group that smells it then they are probably having a micro-seizure in the olfactory part of the brain, which is in charge of processing smells. Think about those patients who claim that they see something or someone, only for the nurse to just dismiss it due to pre-existing medical conditions, which may be inducing hallucinations. But what if it *wasn't* a hallucination; what if there was genuinely something there that the nurse simply couldn't see?

The specialty hospitals, such as psychiatric wards and tuberculosis hospitals, have an even greater chance of being haunted than a regular hospital does. The conditions in psychiatric hospitals that were operating years and years ago were inhumane, to say the least. Patients would be locked in small rooms and sometimes even chained to the wall. Then the doctors would perform horrible procedures, such as lobotomies. When they would perform this procedure the doctor would usually take a very long thin metal rod and put it up the patient's nose and continually ram it around. That would destroy the frontal lobe of the brain and most of the time make the patient a zombie, if it didn't kill them. Then they started using electricity to try to cure these poor people, shocking patients over and over repeatedly, at incrementally higher doses each time. Now that these hospitals are abandoned, all of that trauma and energy of the patients who were experimented on (many of whom died there) remains. This can make it a little more dangerous since the spirits that may still be there were deranged in life, and are probably even worse in death. They could be wandering the halls when suddenly new people show up with all kinds of weird objects, walking around with things in their hands that may remind them of those experiments.

The tuberculosis hospitals are very similar. The difference is that these patients were usually sane, but had a much higher death rate. In these hospitals, the doctors also conducted experiments such as deflating lungs, or even taking parts of the lung out. Deaths occurred on a daily basis in tuberculosis sanatoriums and hospitals. The trauma and multiple deaths that took place on those properties could be the reasons why these facilities undergo so much paranormal activity.

Hospitals are huge places and are easy to get lost in, even when the facility is still in operation. Now, imagine those big hospitals being dark and completely empty. That alone will put people in an uncomfortable position, and that is when the mind starts to play tricks. Every noise seems to be close to you, and does not seem to be a normal noise for the building that you are in—or so you think. Once it gets dark, you will start seeing shadows or light play; either way, you become overwhelmed and very spooked, hearing and seeing things that you wouldn't normally notice. For paranormal investigators, those are the things that we live for, but for others, this is often simply too much to handle.

Chris Balassone, EMT-Paramedic,
director, Tri-City Paranormal,
lecturer and paranormal investigator,
Colonial Heights, Virginia

INTRODUCTION

When we consider what has taken place behind the closed doors of hospitals since the inception of the medical profession, it should come as no surprise to discover that so many of them turn out to be haunted. The typical hospital happens to be a microcosm of the very best and worst extremes of the human experience, providing the perfect stage for the high drama, which tends to occur in even the most stable life at some point in time.

Love. Hate. Fear. Anger. Excitement. Relief. Heartbreak. Depression. Anxiety. All of these, and so many more emotions, are played out against the backdrop of a house of healing. Human beings enter the world in the labor and delivery departments, often kicking and screaming, born in a welter of blood, pain, and blinding light, delivered into the reassuringly stable hands of doctors and nurses.

Others are rushed there by paramedics such as myself, their bodies broken and bleeding; some are shot, stabbed, or otherwise brutalized by the events of a largely uncaring world. My colleagues and I do our best to keep them alive and stabilized as best we can while the lights flash and sirens wail, before entrusting their care to the highly skilled trauma teams who will do their best to save yet another human life.

And finally, hospitals are where so many breathe their last breath. Surrounded by family, friends, and caregivers, a hospital bed is often the place in which the final scenes of a human life are played out, the last lines of that particular book are written, before the cover is closed and the person moves on to whatever it is that comes next.

Life, death, and the entire spectrum of human experience that lies in between those two end points...just another day in the life of a hospital facility.

For the doctors, nurses, therapists, and technicians who have made it their life's work to ease the pain and suffering of their fellow human beings, medicine is a calling—something that they feel drawn to. Medicine is not simply a job or a career choice. It is a *vocation*. The first pair of hands that bring a new life into this world typically belong to a physician; it is often also the hands of a physician that are the last to be laid upon a dying body when that human being leaves this world at the end of their lifetime.

I have made my living as a paramedic and as a clinical educator for many years. It's a profession that I am extremely honored to be a part of, and I feel truly fortunate to do what I do. But my other great passion has always been paranormal investigation. Stories of ghosts and haunted houses have fascinated me for as long as I can remember. As a small boy, I would look forward to visiting my grandparents' house—haunted by several ghosts, including the phantom of an old lady renowned for tucking up children tightly in their beds after the lights went out—with an equal mixture of exhilaration and dread.

Things haven't changed much since then. All these years later, whenever I'm zipping up my equipment packs before heading out to spend the night in some reputedly haunted place, I feel that same level of excitement. Much of the fear has gone, but not *all* of it. Some of the most haunted buildings that I have ever been privileged to set foot in have been hospitals, and paradoxically, some of the best-kept secret ghost stories are from the same kinds of places. After all, what sensible healthcare manager wants to publicize the possibility that their place of healing could be haunted? There is a very reasonable concern about upsetting the patients, or their families, in the very environment where they should feel most relaxed and restful.

But for most of those medical professionals who believe in such things as the paranormal (many doctors simply refuse to even acknowledge the possibility of ghosts being real), it is easiest to adopt a simple "that's just the way it is" attitude, and go on about their business of caring for patients, taking the ghostly goings-on in their stride.

A great example of this involves a local hospital that I once used to transport patients to and from. In all the years that I went in and out of that facility, I never heard the slightest rumor of a ghost story. Not even a hint. When the hospital subsequently closed down, having moved on to a brand new campus elsewhere, I happened to be having dinner with an old friend who once served there as a nurse.

"Of course," she said matter-of-factly, spearing another forkful of pasta. "You know about the doors up on the second floor, right?"

I shook my head, suddenly riveted.

"Oh, they used to open and close themselves all the time on the night shifts. We just used to tell whoever or whatever it was to knock it off once it got to be too annoying, and they always did."

The easy answer would be that it was simply a mechanical problem, of course, but she assured me that the maintenance staff had checked them over thoroughly and found nothing wrong. She and her fellow nurses had simply come to accept that "the resident ghost was up to its tricks again."

Keep calm and carry on, as the saying goes—and if any phrase typifies the profession of nursing, that would be the one. For its practitioners, a haunted hospital is simply business as usual.

Many people believe that ghosts tend to arise in places where death has taken place, and there is much evidence to support that particular contention. But it is also fair to say that some spirits return to places in which they were emotionally invested during their life-time, especially those places in which they experienced either great happiness or sadness. Consider the numerous cases of ghostly nurses and doctors who are still making their rounds, sometimes many decades (in some instances, even *centuries*) after passing away; or the patients who seem to linger on after their deaths, walking the halls and rooms of the hospitals in which they stayed.

I recently had the good fortune to investigate an abandoned former hospital in Utah, where (among many other ghosts) I learned that one of the rooms was said to be haunted by the ghost of a former patient. This tragic soul suffered from the cruel and debilitating disease known as Alzheimer's, a malady that strips away the sufferer's dignity and personality in the worst way imaginable. According to the owners of the former hospital (now converted into a Halloween haunted house), the spirit of this kindly old man returns with some frequency to the room in which he spent many of his final days upon this Earth, interacting with staff and paranor-mal investigators alike on occasion. Those who have encountered this ghost say that it appears to be prone to the sudden and unpre-dictable emotional swings that characterized his behavior in life; if true, what might that say about the survival of consciousness after death? Is it possible that we might take some of our disease pro-cesses with us? Most psychic mediums state emphatically that this is *not* the case, but who can truly say for sure until we each find out the answer for ourselves?

Wandering the long-abandoned hallways and patient care rooms of a massive sanatorium just last week, I was struck by the sense of sheer melancholy that pervaded every single brick of the place. Tens of thousands of people had died in that particular hospital over the years when it served as a fortress on the front lines of America's war against tuberculosis. So great was the rate of patient loss that a body chute was used to transport the bodies of the newly deceased in a discreet manner, affording them a little additional dignity in death and at the same time helping to reduce the drop in morale experienced by those remaining patients who would otherwise be spectators to a seemingly endless parade of body bags passing them by.

With death and suffering having taken place on such a monumental scale, it is no wonder that some trace, some essence of it has remained throughout the years, perhaps imprinted on the very structure of the hospital itself. No wonder then, that such a place should be the scene of phantom footsteps, disembodied voices, mysterious shadow figures, and a host of other paranormal phenomena, all reported by scores of reliable witnesses.

Nor is it just the hospital facilities that cater to diseases and injuries of the body that are prone to being haunted—we must also take into account those that deal primarily with the human brain and mind. And so it is that mental health care institutions (once referred to in a crueler turn of phrases as "madhouses," or the only slightly more palatable term "asylums") also have their ghosts. Patients were often locked up in such places for years on end, if not decades in some cases, sometimes in conditions that bordered upon the inhumane. Procedures such as frontal lobotomies performed with ice picks and hammers were commonplace, inducing some of the most horrific symptoms and side effects in the misguided quest to restore sanity to those judged insane.

Hauntings of mental institutions tend to be rather disturbing in nature, perhaps a reflection of the torment endured by the residents of such facilities. Some poor souls spent the majority of their lives incarcerated, sometimes on the flimsiest of pretexts—if a husband wanted an easy divorce, it was not beyond the realms of possibility to have his wife declared insane, having her carted off quickly and conveniently to the closest institution, perhaps never to see the freedom of the outside world ever again.

Such misery abides, leaving behind a permanent mark or stain upon its environment, perhaps to be experienced again and again by those with suitable abilities and temperament, when the conditions are right for them to do so.

This book does not attempt to be an exhaustive catalogue of every single haunted hospital in the world. Determining precisely which of them are the *most* haunted hospitals is a tall order by itself, and I don't claim to have written the last word on the subject. After all, do we define "most haunted" as the hospitals that are currently still standing and are still under investigation, or do we look at some of those fascinating historical ghost stories and incorporate them into the mix?

The answer is, of course, a little of both. Whenever possible, I have spoken to the people who have actually spent time in those locations, with the goal of conjuring up the atmosphere of those haunted places for you, the reader. What did it *feel* like to encounter the long-dead, ghostly patients and care providers of yesteryear?

We will also spend some time delving into the fascinating histories of our chosen hospitals. The details of a haunting are only half the story. It is also vitally important to ask *why* the place might be haunted. Sometimes, events that took place on the land itself before the medical facility was even a daydream in the mind of its architect can answer that crucial question, or can at least lead us further down the path that leads toward the truth. It is for this reason that some of the hospitals contained within this book are the focus of just one or two resident ghosts, whereas others are home to many times that number. In selecting the locations, I have gone for what I believe to be the most interesting stories, not for sheer volume alone. Where possible, I have interviewed those who have actually spent time in the haunted hospitals. When that has not been possible, it has been necessary to rely upon written or video sources of information.

Many of these stories are extraordinary, standing in defiance of all conventional logic. Those of an overly skeptical nature may find them difficult or impossible to believe. With the passage of time, it is difficult to know precisely where fact leaves off and where folklore begins. So, *caveat emptor*: let the buyer beware. If you have any additional information about the medical facilities and associated hauntings contained within this book, please feel free to contact me via my website—*www.richardestep.net*—and I will be happy to make corrections in future editions of the book.

And so...

The first hands that ever held you.

The last hands that will ever touch you.

There is a good chance that one or both will take place within the walls of a hospital. *Of course* they have their ghosts. . . .

Would you care to go and meet some of them?

Asylum 49
(Formerly the Tooele Hospital)
Utah, USA

If a building could ever be described as being schizophrenic, then that building would be the old Tooele Hospital. Located in the city of Tooele, less than an hour's drive away from Salt Lake City, one half of the building is an abandoned medical care facility that has been turned into a fright-based haunted house attraction. The *other* half is a fully functional retirement home for senior citizens. The fact that these two wildly different worlds are able to co-exist in relative harmony is surprising, to say the least—the only thing that separates them is a single doorway between the new wing and the old one.

Originally built in 1873 by a man named Samuel Lee, the building was a family residence for 40 years before passing into the hands of the county in 1913, when it was pressed into service as a care home for senior citizens and those with special needs. Its nickname during that era speaks volumes, as locals referred to it as "the county poor house." Mr. Lee and his young son Thomas are said to be just two of the many ghosts who haunt the corridors and bedrooms of this historic old structure. At approximately seven years of age, Thomas is said to be a playful and mischievous (though harmless) young spirit who takes great delight in playing games with the flesh and blood staff and residents of the nursing facility, not to mention those who visit its haunted house alter ego in the hopes of getting a good scare.

After closing its doors as a hospital for the last time, the old building has had occasional brushes with fame by serving as a TV and movie set, including the acclaimed TV miniseries adaption of Stephen King's *The Stand,* where it stood in for the very real Boulder Community Hospital during filming.

Entrepreneurs Kimm and Cami Andersen created the medically themed Halloween-style haunted house known as *Asylum 49* in 2006, complete with its own ambulances, which are sometimes crewed by demonic-looking paramedics and doctors. It also doesn't hurt in the least bit that the building sits directly adjacent to the local cemetery! Starting out with an extremely skeptical attitude, the Andersens quickly became convinced that their new investment was a haunted house in more than name only.

A number of psychic mediums have visited throughout the years, and have made some remarkable claims about the place. Perhaps the most intriguing one is that the old Tooele Hospital contains a portal to another dimension, over which a ghostly nurse named Maria is said to stand guard, warning away the spirits of newly deceased residents from taking the wrong path into the afterlife.

A far more disturbing aspect of the haunting is the reported presence of a frightening man in black. This shadow figure, said to be

The old Tooele Hospital and its ambulances.

malicious, is seen wandering the hallways after dark and is a source of great trepidation for those who have encountered him. This shadow man is most commonly seen at three o'clock in the morning. Nurses have witnessed this apparition walk across the hallway and pass directly through a closed door, which turned out to be locked from the inside. Getting no answer from the patient inside the room, the frightened night duty nurse summoned a maintenance man to remove the door from its hinges. Both the nurse and the maintenance man were shocked to find that the occupant of the room, who had been visited by the black shadow figure, had died earlier that night.

The ghost of a young girl has also been seen. At first, she seemed localized to one specific conference room in the condemned hospital wing, but when the Asylum 49 haunted house opened its doors for business, customers often claimed that the scariest part of the attraction was the young girl who followed them around from room to room. Staff didn't always have the heart to tell them that there *was* no young girl working at Asylum 49. Perhaps the most frightening aspect of the haunting of this former hospital is the belief commonly held by the nursing staff that the appearance of this ghostly young child presages the death within the building.

In 2011, Zak Bagans and his *Ghost Adventures* crew spent the night locked down in Asylum 49, where they experienced what appears to be some fascinating potentially paranormal activity.

When Bagans and his crew interviewed the current nursing home staff on camera, these trained medical professionals were not shy about recounting their own ghostly encounters within the building. For example, the sound of what the staff presumed to be an escaped patient was heard walking back and forth across the roof at 4:30 one morning—which was completely empty.

A team of local paranormal investigators named the *Utah Ghost Organization*, who were conducting an EVP session in the building, received a class A EVP (class A EVPs are the best and clearest possible type of electronic voice phenomenon, believed to be the voice of a deceased person), which clearly stated the name of an x-ray technician who used to work at the hospital. This finding was eerily mirrored by the *Ghost Adventures* crew during their own night at the Tooele hospital when they also received a class A EVP, which quite clearly said the name "Zak Bagans." The *Ghost Adventures* boys also captured what they believe to be a hostile, verbally abusive male voice growling at them in one of the Asylum 49 rooms, and then later speaking directly into Bagans's ear. Similarly crude EVPs were recorded on the team's digital voice recorders. A high-pitched female scream was also picked up by the *Ghost Adventures* team, in addition to a forlorn, almost child-like moan, which was captured on an old-style reel-to-reel analog tape recorder.

Using heat-sensitive thermal imaging cameras, Bagans and his team also captured an intriguing heat anomaly, which came into view and then disappeared almost instantaneously. Also recorded on camera was a ball that was being used as a control object, which subsequently rolled down the corridor toward their locked-off video camera. Bagans believed that this could have been a manifestation of the two child-like shadow figures that he had seen standing right next to him, playfully moving the ball around for fun.

During their lockdown, the *Ghost Adventures* crew also witnessed doors slamming inside empty rooms, footsteps were heard in deserted hallways, and investigator Aaron Goodwin claimed that he was grabbed on the hip by an unseen hand.

Bagans theorized that the old hospital is now basically a "ghost-manufacturing factory," especially considering the fact that elderly inhabitants are still passing away there on a regular basis.

Whether you buy into Zak Bagans's theories or not, there is no doubt that something strange and mysterious is afoot inside Asylum 49, and I was sufficiently intrigued to find out for myself. Kimm and Cami Andersen were more than willing to let me and a couple of fellow investigators from my team, the Boulder County Paranormal Research Society, spend a night there and take a look at the place firsthand. On a bright and sunny Saturday morning in May, we loaded up our trucks and took Interstate-25 north out of Colorado. Our little two-vehicle convoy headed west through Wyoming and into Utah, putting more than 500 miles of empty prairie behind us in the rear-view mirror. When we hit Salt Lake City, ominous grey thunderclouds were hanging low in the sky. No sooner had I thought that it might rain, than the heavens opened and fat drops of rain started to spatter across my windshield as I drove the final leg of the journey into Tooele.

So many scary movies and stories begin with "it was a dark and stormy night," but it's rarely true of my real-life paranormal investigations. Tooele was very much the exception. Pulling into the parking lot at Asylum 49, it felt like the perfect night for something paranormal to manifest itself.

Because the daylight was starting to melt away into the gloom of twilight, we wasted no time pulling out our cameras and circling the entire building, snapping photographs of the exterior. Working our way to the rear of the structure, we came upon some abandoned medical office buildings and then a very neatly kept cemetery, the same one that I had seen Zak Bagans interview Kimm Andersen in during the *Ghost Adventures* TV episode. A disembodied hand clawing its way up out of the ground gave me the shock of my life, until I realized that it was nothing more than a latex prop, the sort that can be bought at a Halloween store. We left it for the next unwary traveler to enjoy!

Kimm, Cami, and their staff were warm, friendly, and very welcoming. Kimm was hard at work on construction of the building— Asylum 49 is a constant work-in-progress, as the Andersens strive to make it better and better with every passing season—but took a break to fill us in on some of the background to the case. Cami escorted us on a tour throughout the building, pointing out the areas of interest and the specific haunted hot spots.

Starting with the north wing, we turned a corner that led into the maternity area, only to come face-to-face with a life-sized "Human Centipede"—three dummies positioned nose-to-tail in the most disturbing way (I'm not going to lie; I jumped halfway out of my skin when I saw it). "We go where other haunted houses don't dare," Cami laughed. She wasn't kidding. During the course of our tour, we encountered a crashed UFO complete with a snarling alien crew and eggs that oozed slime; a disturbing array of surgical oddities, such as dismembered bodies sewn together in a sinister tableaux that looked as though they had been pieced together by a deranged anatomist; and evil experiments conducted by a surgical team from Hell upon an unwilling, bedbound victim. All of this was barely scratching the surface. I don't want to give away all of Asylum 49's spooky secrets, but suffice it to say that it isn't a place for the faint of heart!

We heard about the impressions given by a number of mediums and people claiming psychic abilities who have visited Asylum 49. The resident spirits, they said, included at least one doctor and nurse, a pair of little girls named Tabitha and Sarah, and one adult spirit who is both deaf and unable to speak. Cami has personally seen the apparitions of Tabitha, the doctor, and the nurse.

I should mention that during this interview with Kimm and Cami we were standing in the same location that doubled as the baby ward of Boulder Community Hospital in the TV miniseries adaptation of Stephen King's *The Stand*, something that my inner geek found to be extremely cool.

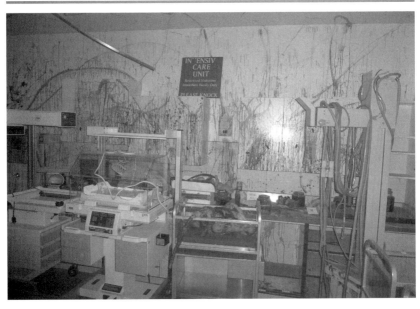

Asylum 49's Intensive Care Unit, where numerous ghostly experiences have been reported.

"This hospital was sort of known as the hospital of death," Cami said bluntly. "Nobody would come here if they could help it, for a combination of reasons. This is a small town, and the hospital was built mainly because there are a lot of military bases around here."

The Andersens have been running a haunted house in the city of Tooele for a decade now. "All the spirits here know what we do," explained Cami as she led us deeper into the building. "They like to peek in and sometimes be a part of the show. Sarah especially likes to scare the customers. I see her every year. She looks like the girl from the movie *The Grudge,* very pale with dark brown hair."

Kimm broke in to describe some of the evidence that he and Cami have gathered during their time running Asylum 49. He believes that the reason for them being able to gather such a wealth of fascinating results is that the Andersens have built and nurtured a relationship with the paranormal residents of the building, particularly because they both spend so many of their waking hours inside there doing renovation work.

While conducting his own amateur ghost hunt with some friends and family, a Serbian friend of Kimm's captured an extraordinary photograph in the main hallway late one night, containing what appeared to be the form of a man at the end of the empty corridor. "I can see you!" the ghost hunter exclaimed. "What is your name?"

The voice box that he was carrying immediately piped up with, "My name is Robert."

Robert happened to be the name of a shadow figure that was well known by the Asylum 49 staff to haunt that very same hallway. But Robert isn't alone, and the figure captured by the Serbian's digital camera isn't him. When zooming in to blow up the facial features, they appear to be somewhat...*unnatural* in appearance, as though the man is wearing a mask of some kind. In fact, the features look decidedly clown-like, an opinion that Kimm went on to voice several times after the picture was taken.

Accompanying a medium through the building one day, Kimm was not thrilled to hear that there was a spirit lurking in the hallway that was less than happy with her. "The spirit says that you make fun of him," the medium continued. "He says that you call him a...a *clown,* or something?"

"The clown guy!" Kimm suddenly realized.

"His face looks like that because of how he died," explained the medium. "He died in a fire."

Shadow forms and figures are nothing new at Asylum 49. They crop up regularly on both the in-house security video system and on the cameras brought by visitors. One particularly chilling piece of video footage was taken in an area of the building that has been informally dubbed the "scary hallway" by Asylum 49 staff. A shadowy figure can clearly be seen lurking at the back of a guided tour group as it makes its way along the corridor, a ghostly hanger-on captured for posterity by a video camera.

Passing through what had once been the patient rooms, I made the observation that the beds looked old enough to have been the original hospital beds, which Cami confirmed. The Andersens both feel that because there are still residents at the hospital (the spirits who have remained there) they would like to retain as many of the fixtures and fittings as possible. For instance one of the rooms is haunted by the ghost of an older lady who likes to stimulate EMF meter readings when a deck of cards is brought out.

In the central hallway from which many of the rooms branch off, paranormal investigators have captured video footage of a shadowy figure walking into one of the rooms. We stopped at the door to the room, which is said to be haunted by a patient named Wes, who suffered from the cruel and debilitating conditions known as Alzheimer's and schizophrenia. A visiting medium stated that this particular ghost was still earthbound due to the fact that he died in a state of confusion. Although, if true, that would beg the question of why the millions of people who die in a state of confusion do not remain behind as ghosts.

I told Cami that my fellow paranormal investigators and I do not believe in provocation as a means of stimulating an interaction with ghosts due to its disrespectful nature, however, we do favor encouragement—inviting them to touch us somewhere, for example. She cautioned us that Wes and some of the other residents of Asylum 49 have been known to respond by scratching and pinching overly provocative investigators. I pondered this warning thoughtfully as I stood outside Wes's room, looking at the pencil sketch of him drawn by one of the visiting psychics: a placid-looking older man with a bald head and a level gaze stared back at me from the drawing that was placed outside his door.

The former doctors' lounge was known for having an inhospitable atmosphere, reinforced by the fact that on one occasion when Cami was vacuuming, a voice had barked at her to "get out!" Moving into the x-ray room, we heard of the resident spirit there, a former technician who had worked at the hospital during its heyday and despite not having died on the premises, seemed to have returned to the place he loved working at after his death. The tech had given his full name to investigators in the form of an EVP, which I heard for myself and found to be extremely compelling. A check of records corroborated this man's name. This is an intelligent facet of the haunt that loves to interact with living visitors of Asylum 49, and it is far from the only one.

"This is the Guardian's area," Cami said, referring to the part of the hospital that was close to the entrance doors. We pushed our way through what seemed like hundreds of trash bags suspended from the ceiling, making a dark and claustrophobic maze. This room had been the MRI chamber when the hospital was still open. "He's big. He's grumpy. And he will mess with you a lot, especially your equipment. For example, when Jay from *Ghost Mine* was here, his K-2 meter was in the red all the time. There are no electrical sources back here to explain it. We believe that the Guardian could be behind the physical attacks on investigators that have taken place in this area."

Entering the mirror maze, we were surrounded by reflections of reflections of reflections of ourselves on every surface, and warned about the resident male ghost that liked to grab female visitors on inappropriate parts of their body. Cami showed us a photo taken by a female visitor to the maze, which—though nothing unusual had been seen at the time—showed what looked like faces and figures staring back from the depths of one of the mirrors. It would be easy to dismiss them as pareidolia (the brain's tendency to see human faces and forms in natural patterns of light as they play across surfaces), but the level of detail was a little too sharp for my liking.

Unsurprisingly, although paranormal activity takes place at Asylum 49 all year round, it is at its very height during late October, when the commercial haunted house is in full swing. Hordes of visitors, eager to experience the thrills and chills cooked up by the Andersens and their dedicated staff, bring along with them a tsunami of emotional energy, something upon which the spirits seem able to draw. In the 2014 Halloween season, more than 38,000 visitors came through the doors of Asylum 49—and that is a *lot* of energy.

Kimm had rolled a number of hospital beds out into the hallway shortly before opening the doors to the public, placed mannequins on each one, and covered the fake bodies up with white sheets. This created a rather creepy hallway of cadavers. Satisfied with his work, Kimm was just about to head over to the main entrance to get the evening rolling when he stopped suddenly. There, standing in the doorway of patient room #2, was the apparition of a little girl. He could see her as plain as day. The girl was completely solid, wearing a full-length lace dress. Long brown hair fell down over her shoulders.

The girl had both hands over her eyes, and she was crying. Kimm could not only see her, he could hear her sobbing.

"It's not fair...it's not fair..." the girl repeated, over and over again.

Sarah was putting in an appearance.

This little girl usually manifested in either the nursery or, like tonight, patient room #2. She liked to hide in a nook between the rocking chair and heater in the nursery, and had been seen there by quite a few staff and visitors to the old hospital over the years.

Engaging her in conversation despite the outlandishness of the situation, Kimm was told that Sarah was unhappy because she wanted to join in with the colorfully clothed, blood-splattered actors who were about to scare the patrons halfway out of their wits. Thinking quickly, Kimm asked the ghostly little child to hide underneath the beds out in the hallway and snatch at the feet of the passers-by. Nodding her agreement, Sarah then faded to black and disappeared before Kimm's astonished eyes.

"Still, to this day, I get huge bumps every time I talk about her," he told me with a visible shudder. From that point on, Asylum 49 staff would catch glimpses of a black mist, moving from bed to bed to bed in that very same corridor.

Our own night there turned out to be rather interesting. Although nothing of note was captured during an EVP session that we conducted in Wesley's room, we did get strong K2 EMF meter hits in there when I offered to share my turkey sandwich with him, and also when a colleague asked him about his sports team preferences.

We tried another EVP session over in the nursery, where Sarah likes to hang out. Once again, although no paranormal voices were recorded, our REM-POD EMF meter would go crazy, lighting up over and over again, as if in the presence of an unseen energy source of some kind. There were no artificial power sources that could have explained it, and the entire group had switched our phones off at the beginning of the investigation. The reason for the REM-POD's anomalous behavior has still not been satisfactorily explained.

Back in the days when Asylum 49 was a functioning hospital, the boardroom was the place in which decisions both large and small were made concerning the hospital's future. Now, row upon row of white cloaked, hooded figures sat in church pews staring back at my team and me as we clustered around the board table, which was covered with K2 meters, REM-PODs, and a host of other accoutrements of the paranormal investigator's trade. Remembering a warning given by our tour guide Misty earlier on that same evening ("these figures sometimes move all by themselves") I kept a watchful eye on this silent gallery of observers, while Kimm told us about the two resident boardroom spirits, a pair of ghostly children by the

These hooded figures move of their own accord in what was once the hospital boardroom.

names of Christian and Jessica. Christian is believed to be two years old, and Jessica is thought to be seven, if what the psychic mediums have stated is accurate.

Both children are extremely playful, liking nothing more than to play pranks on visitors and staff alike. My team and I listened intently to an EVP captured in that same board room, in which a young girl's voice says, "I'm here...now." The voice rasps in much the same way that any child does when it is play-acting a monster. Another EVP, also very easy to hear, can quite clearly be heard to say "Mom?" and "Yeah."

Not all EVPs captured at Asylum 49 are quite as benign. Kimm and Cami regularly inform visitors that before leaving (whether they have any spiritual beliefs or not), to speak with intent to any spirits within earshot and tell them in no uncertain terms that they are not permitted to accompany them in the car or to follow them home. Despite that, one chilling EVP was captured in which an adult female voice quite plainly states: "I'm going with you." Another says bluntly: "You're dead."

Sobering words indeed. On leaving the old hospital under a cloudy early morning sky, I made a point to follow Kimm and Cami's advice, stating quite firmly and forcefully that *nobody* was welcome to accompany me on the long drive back to Colorado.

It remains to be seen whether they actually listened.

RAF Hospital Nocton Hall
Lincolnshire, United Kingdom

Both a priory and a manor house once occupied the grounds on which the burned-out shell of this once proud and mighty manor house now stands. Its predecessor, Nocton Old Hall, went up in flames in the year 1834, and so it is then that the mysterious history of Nocton Hall was born in the aftermath of one great fire, and tragically seems to have ended its life in the flames of another.

First built in 1841 as a home for the Earl of Ripon, Nocton Hall has seen more than its share of trauma over the course of its lifetime—trauma of both the physical and the emotional kind. When the United States allied with Great Britain during World War I, the British Government allowed the U.S. Army to use Nocton Hall as a place of rest and recuperation for the soldiers returning from the horrific battlefields of Europe. It was a place of peaceful contemplation, rest, and reflection for many of these young officers during the final two years of the war, a significant number of whom would be carrying the burden of post-traumatic stress disorder in addition to the more visible wounds that they had received in combat.

Nobody seemed to know what to do with the hall after "the war to end all wars" was over, and so Nocton languished for the better part of 20 years. But with a new menace on the rise in the form of Hitler's Nazi Germany, it soon became apparent to the Air Ministry that Britain was likely to find herself embroiled in another European war in the very near future. Foreseeing the need for more hospital facilities to meet the increasing needs of the burgeoning Royal Air Force ranks, those in charge decided to repurpose Nocton Hall as a medical hospital. By happenstance, there were a large concentration of air bases in the county of Lincolnshire, and only one hospital currently capable of serving them all, so this solution made perfect sense.

Nocton Hall in it's prime, circa 1901. Photo credit: Wikimedia Commons

As World War II spread, America entered the war on the side of the Allied powers, just as she had done during the Great War. Nocton Hall was given over to the United States military once more, becoming the U.S. Army's Seventh General Hospital.

After the surrender of Germany and Japan, Nocton was returned to British hands, becoming No. 1 Royal Air Force Hospital Nocton Hall. The site was expanded upon, with new specialist wards and clinical capacities added to it. By the 1950s, not only was a dental clinic in operation there, but a maternity ward was also installed. At the height of its productivity, Nocton had the capacity for more than 740 patients, making it a major healthcare facility of its time. In 1983, even as the Cold War was reaching its peak, the Thatcher government made the unpopular decision to close down the hospital, feeling that the money could be better spent elsewhere.

Fortunately, the United States was once again ready to step in and help to keep Nocton Hall going, leasing it from the British government as a "standby hospital"—a facility intended to be kept basically in mothballs, but ready to be brought back to life in the event of a major war. And war did indeed eventually come, not in the expected form of Red Army tank divisions rolling into West Germany, but rather in the unanticipated guise of Iraqi tanks invading the tiny Persian Gulf nation of Kuwait, acting on the orders of dictator Saddam Hussein. As America and her allies began to deploy hundreds of thousands of military personnel to the Persian Gulf as part of *Operation Desert Shield* (soon to become *Operation Desert Storm*) future allied casualties were expected to be potentially massive. Armchair pundits at the time predicted that the liberation of Kuwait could be a bloodbath.

United States Air Force medical personnel were flown to Nocton Hall from their home base in California, establishing what came to be known as the 310th Contingency Hospital. Fortunately, the much-feared tsunami of casualties never materialized—just 35 patients were treated there, easily handled by the 1,300 medical professionals staffing the hospital.

When the Gulf War was over, and the need for this particular hospital had diminished once more, a skeleton crew of just 13 American service personnel remained stationed at Nocton Hall in order to oversee the upkeep of the facility; but after finally handing it back once more to the British government in 1994, Nocton was finally closed down and soon abandoned, left to stand empty while a new owner was vainly sought.

The wire fence that was placed around the shell of the grand old house after it was finally closed has been penetrated by countless vandals and arsonists throughout the years, many of whom have defaced its brick walls and stonework with graffiti, and set much of what remains of the leftover furniture on fire. Indeed, a series of small fires charred and blackened several parts of the building. This despicable criminal behavior reached a climax just before midnight on October 24, 2004, when a major conflagration swept through the Hall, completely gutting the interior. Fortunately, the responding firefighters were able to save the structure itself, although the burned, water-weakened roof caved in, collapsing down into the upper floors. Nocton Hall was tragically left a smoldering, ruined shadow of its former glory, unwanted by the living and therefore entrusted into the keeping of its resident ghosts.

Tenants of the hall throughout the years—usually nurses or patients—have long told stories of a phantom grey lady, seen gliding silently along the corridors and hallways in the early morning hours. Why she should haunt the building is a mystery, which remains unsolved to this day. But what is by far the most frequently reported ghost at Nocton Hall makes for a much more tragic figure, and embodies a dark and disturbing legend.

Primarily associated with one specific residential room, the apparition of a young lady has been seen by multiple occupants, her appearance always contriving to wake them up at the stroke of four-thirty in the morning. This miserable young specter cries forlornly, deeply upset by her mistreatment at the hands of a former lover. Although her identity is not known for certain, the manner of her dress would suggest that she was a household servant in a bygone age. Those who have paid attention to the words that are interspersed with her sobs have said that she weeps so bitterly because the young master of the house, having worked his way into her affections—although some darker versions of the story claim that he in fact forced himself upon her—took advantage of the naïve young lady. When their illicit meetings resulted in the servant becoming pregnant, the young "gentleman" arranged to have her murdered in cold blood.

Did this actually happen? Does the grief-stricken soul of a murdered serving girl truly haunt her former room at Nocton Hall?

The burned-out ruins of 21st-century Nocton Hall. Photo credit: Wikicommons user Now3d.

Historical records are unclear on the matter, but one fascinating incident came to the attention of the world media in 2013, which *may* shed some more light on the matter. Reporter Graham Newton of the *Grantham Journal* published an article titled "Ghost turns up on Grantham urban explorer's photo." The article recounts the story of two friends who had visited Nocton Hall one night, with the purposes of exploring the dusty remnants of its corridors and rooms. When an urban explorer named Louise Lewin took a photograph of her companion John down in the cellar at roughly nine-thirty, she noticed nothing unusual at all—just John posing in a doorway, standing perfectly still in the dim light.

It was only afterward, when she had posted the photo on her social media page that events took a turn toward the bizarre. Friends who posted comments on her Facebook wall thought that they could see a figure dressed in white, standing next to John on his left side.

"It looks like she is walking next to John and trying to link arms with him. When you zoom in her mouth is open and it looks like she is crying,"[1] Louise said.

I encourage you to seek out the photo online and judge for yourself. Is this a human figure, approximately 5 feet high, standing next to John in the doorway—or simply pareidolia, the tendency of the human mind to see faces and figures that aren't really there, due to the interplay of light and shadow across different surfaces? You be the judge.

Ghosts of a different kind would come to Nocton Hall in November of 2013, when a movie crew arrived to shoot scenes for the horror movie *The Woman in Black 2: Angel of Death*. One is forced to wonder what the ghosts of the grey lady and the weeping girl would have made of their black-garbed Hollywood counterpart....

According to British national newspaper *The Daily Mail*, Nocton Hall is now listed as one of the United Kingdom's 10 most endangered historic buildings.[2] A movement is underway to raise funds in order to save the building, and also to hopefully renovate it, restoring it to at least some semblance of its former glory. If the campaign is successful—as I truly hope that it is—then perhaps you will get the chance to spend a night there...in which case, I strongly suggest that you choose your room carefully, and keep your eyes firmly open when the clock strikes half past four....

The Clark Air Base Hospital
Luzon Island, Philippines

One of the world's most heavily populated islands and home to approximately 50 million people, Luzon lies at the heart of the chain of islands known as the Philippines. The Philippines have long played a pivotal role in United States military strategy, with American troops and other service personnel being stationed there throughout most of the 20th century.

In 1903, President Franklin Delano Roosevelt would sign the executive order leading to the establishment of U.S. Army Fort Stotsenburg, three miles west of Angelo City. One major reason for choosing this particular location was that the grass made good feed for the cavalry horses. Military aviation was still in its infancy during the early 1900s, but was rapidly gaining interest and growing in popularity in the army and navy (the U.S. Air Force would not be formed for four more decades). Like many major military bases of the time, Fort Stotsenburg possessed a dedicated airstrip, primarily operated by the Army Signal Corps. In 1919, in keeping with the long-established military tradition of naming new installations after prominent members of the service, the Army Signal Corps named the fledgling new air field Clark Field after Signal Corps Major Harold Clark.

The American military establishment was not blind to the steady growth and increasing reach of the Japanese war machine. As the 1930s gave way to the 1940s, more and more American bomber squadrons were transferred to Clark Field. Following the Japanese sneak attack on the fleet at Pearl Harbor on the morning of Sunday, December 7, 1941, the flames of war engulfed the entire Pacific region. Clark Field was subject to a massive Japanese air strike on December 8, with enemy aircraft raining down bombs upon the hangars and runway alike with impunity. The raid destroyed much of the American bomber force while it was still on the ground. More air raids were to follow.

One story, which still makes the rounds both locally[1] and on a multitude of Internet websites, but has proven difficult to substantiate, tells of a particularly heavy bombing raid during the Christmas holiday season of 1941. The Home Plate Canteen was supposedly bombed when it was full to capacity with service personnel enjoying a holiday dinner—the vast majority of whom were said to be killed. Whether the story is true or not is difficult to say, though it seems odd that base personnel had time to enjoy a holiday dinner when Clark Field was evacuated by December 24 of that year. But a number of local eyewitnesses have reported hearing the distant, haunting melodies of period Swing music playing in the vicinity of what used to be the Home Plate Canteen, particularly in the early hours of the morning. Other passers-by have heard the sounds of animated conversation, laughter, and the sort of general revelry that would suggest either a party or similar social gathering was going on. Few have had the courage to go in any closer, and those who do dare to investigate are never able to find a source for the inexplicable noises.

With defeat almost inevitable, the battered and bloodied American forces ultimately evacuated from Clark, flying out the personnel and as much salvageable equipment as possible on Christmas Eve of 1941. Japanese forces then overran the entire base, occupied it, and made it their own. One fascinating historical footnote, which most people are unaware of, also dates back to this particular time period. Something truly ugly was born at Clark Field when it lay within Japanese hands: the *Kamikaze,* or "divine wind." These one-way suicide missions were first flown out of Clark in 1944, the pilots weaving and twisting their way through the flak screens of U.S. Navy ships before slamming into the decks of the American aircraft carriers and exploding in a ball of fire, immolating the unlucky sailors who happened to be in their path. The Kamikaze pilots were trained in the small town of Mabalcat, which can be found just a couple of miles east of Clark Base. To this day, a historical marker stands outside an anonymous-looking building in the town, commemorating the place in which those pilots prepared themselves for their final, fatal mission.

It would be two long years before the American forces were in a position to strike back at the Japanese forces occupying both Fort Stotsenburg and Clark Field, launching long-range air strikes in an intense bomber campaign that lasted from October of 1944 to January of 1945. More than a thousand Japanese aircraft were destroyed or disabled during that time, blasted into smoldering wreckage by their American counterparts. With the writing truly on the wall for the ailing Japanese military, the installation was finally retaken by the Americans after a few fierce firefights that very same January.

After the war ended, Fort Stotsenburg and Clark Field duly amalgamated and became Clark Air Base. As one of the biggest (arguably *the* biggest) U.S. overseas military installations, thousands of service personnel and their dependents passed through the establishment throughout the years, bringing with them the full gamut of human emotional experience, both good and bad. In order to meet their medical needs, a brand new state-of-the-art healthcare facility was constructed on the base in 1964. The Clark Air Base Hospital saw hundreds of babies brought into the world and, as we shall see, it was the last stop for many of those who were to leave it.

Thousands of civilian patients were treated there each month, including those who sought care at its flourishing dental practice. During the Vietnam War, Clark was a key strategic base, serving not only as a major logistical hub for the American forces, but also as the first point of medical evacuation for troops being flown out of the Vietnamese theater of operation. Clark's hospital wards would become a temporary home to soldiers who had been wounded on the battlefield—some grievously. Bullets, blades, punji sticks, artillery shells, and countless other weapons were capable of inflicting the most horrific injuries imaginable upon the human body, and after stabilization by trauma surgeons in the field tent hospitals, those survivors were shipped back to Clark for more definitive medical care.

It is also important to bear in mind that the physical wounds of war can be matched (if not exceeded) by the psychological injuries, which are harder to find because they have a habit of lurking beneath the surface. What we know today as Post-Traumatic Stress Disorder (PTSD) was referred to during the 1970s as "Vietnam Syndrome." The name was different, but the effects were the same—crippling mental illness brought on by the extreme stresses of combat. The Clark Air Base Hospital did indeed have a mental health ward, but one has to wonder whether it was able to cope with the sheer volume of emotionally traumatized servicemen returning from the front lines. Entire bus-loads of new patients would arrive there every day.

With so much raw emotion, and with so much sheer trauma of both the physical and the psychological kind passing through its doors, is it any wonder that a place such as the Clark Air Base Hospital should become the center of so many ghost stories?

When the volcano Mount Pinatubo erupted violently in 1991, tons of volcanic ash was hurled into the air, carried aloft on the winds, and ignominiously dumped over pretty much all of Clark Air Base. The hospital was hit particularly hard, and when the last American forces took down the Stars and Stripes before departing from Clark that same year, what was once a shining example of modern medical practice was allowed to languish and rot. To add further insult to injury, looters broke into the hospital and completely gutted it, stripping the rooms bare of anything that might hold even the slightest value. This included not only the expensive medical equipment, but fittings and fixtures as simple as door handles and window frames. Like maggots stripping a dead carcass down to its barest bones, the looters kept coming back until absolutely nothing was left but for the structure...and the ghosts.

Although paranormal activity has been reported at several places on the base grounds, such as the auditory phenomena emanating from the old Home Plate Canteen and the ghost of an airman who supposedly hanged himself to avoid falling into Japanese hands and whose restless spirits is now said to haunt the base museum, most of the ghostly episodes seem to center upon the former hospital. But before we investigate the ghostly goings-on at the medical center itself, it is worth taking a little time to consider the hauntings that have brought paranormal enthusiasts from far and wide in order to visit the other areas of this massive military installation.

In an article published in the *Philippine Star* (on Halloween of 2012, appropriately enough) titled "Ghost Tourism drawing visitors to former U.S. base,"[2] journalist Ding Cervantes delves into some of Clark's ghostly activity and paranormal folklore. One such haunting involves the old cemetery, from which bodies were moved to the newer American military cemetery on the airbase in order to allow for redevelopment of a new building on the site of the former graveyard. Construction on the new building was never completed, partly because—according to local chief of tourism Guy Hilbero— "Employees in the area claimed they frequently see ghosts or hear unusual sounds coming from the unfinished building. There's no doubt it is haunted."

In Filipino culture, loud noises are sometimes used to scare off ghosts and spirits, something that Cervantes's article tells us still happens at Clark today in an area that contains some rather unique trees:

Hilbero also noted the Tres Marias (three pine trees)—named "aguso" in the Kapampangan language—found along the road leading to Clark's exit gate in Mabalacat City. "I don't know the history of those three pine trees which can't be found elsewhere in Clark, but the road near them has been the site of several accidents. Motorists are prompted to either honk their horns or make the sign of the cross when passing by," he said.

Lily Hill is the tallest point of land on Clark Air Base, and it saw ferocious combat between American and Japanese ground forces during World War II, serving as the scene of a bitter last stand for the Japanese when U.S. soldiers retook the base. As with so many battlefields, the hill held the reputation of being haunted for many years afterward. How much of that reputation was truly deserved is impossible to say, but it's interesting to note that after a series of religious cleansing ceremonies, locals no longer regard Lily Hill as a haunted place these days.

Although the building that once housed the base hospital is now a gutted shell, a mere shadow of the medical facility that cost more than $4.5 million to build, it is far from a peaceful place. Those who live in the area say that the apparitions of servicemen long dead may sometimes be seen walking through the ruined interior of the abandoned hospital, both by day and by night. Whereas many local residents avoid the area at night, a few adventurous folks (usually teenagers) occasionally venture into the area in an attempt to see whether the ghostly tales have any truth to them. But the real experts on the paranormal activity taking place at the Clark Air Base Hospital are those brave souls who prowl its corridors with a flashlight once darkness has fallen: the night shift security guards. The guards were no stranger to hearing footsteps and voices after dark in the area of the hospital, along with the apparition of a female clad entirely in white who has been seen drifting through the ruins on more than one occasion.

Blogger and urban explorer Robert Joe is a man who likes to find his own answers. Working on behalf of his National Geographic TV show *I Wouldn't Go in There*, Robert set out to spend some time inside the crumbling walls of the former hospital building in order to investigate the ghost stories for himself. But before he stepped foot inside the place, Robert and his production team interviewed a number of former Clark civilian employees, including one of the night watchmen who had patrolled the building on an hourly basis each evening after ten o'clock, back in the 1970s when the hospital was still functioning. One of the most compelling reasons for paranormal activity to take place mostly at night (or, at least, for it to *appear* to take place mostly at night—the jury is still out) is that the world around us is so much quieter and calmer; sounds travel further without the hustle and bustle of the daytime world as a backdrop, allowing smaller and fainter sounds to be heard more easily.

One former Clark Hospital security guard reported hearing the sound of boots striding across the cement floor, followed almost immediately by the sensation of overwhelming coldness blanketing his body when he was patrolling the first floor shortly after midnight. The unfortunate guard then came face to face with the apparition of what appeared to be an American serviceman, large of stature, and uniformed in military camo fatigues. As the security guard's stupefied gaze traveled slowly upward from the serviceman's boots to a point just above his neck, the man was terrified to realize that the only thing missing was the soldier's face.

If this were the "classic" ghostly encounter, whether it happened to be in fact or fiction, this would be the point at which the apparition would fade away into nothingness, leaving the startled witness to question his own sanity. But in this case, something far more interesting happened. The faceless soldier asked for a cigarette. The security guard handed one over with hands that must surely have been trembling with fear. The ghostly soldier physically took the proffered cigarette, causing an icy chill to run through the guard's fingers. It was only then, when the guard had lit the soldier's cigarette for him, that the apparition suddenly disappeared into thin air—body, cigarette, cloud of smoke, and all.

This same security guard also insists that the hospital basement was used as a morgue for the temporary storage of the bodies of men, women, and even children who had died in the hospital. He reported hearing plaintive cries for help from the darkened corners down there. But the American personnel that I contacted who were stationed on the base tell a very different story. According to them, bodies were never kept down in the Clark Hospital basement at all. They were very appropriately buried in the dedicated cemetery on base, which is still there today (and is not even close to being at full capacity).

Based upon his own research, Robert Joe is inclined to agree with them.

The idea of "bodies in the basement" just screams urban legend...it was a modern American military hospital; of course they'd have a regulated and normal method of storing and disposing of bodies. Whether these regulations were stretched during times of stress in war?, I can't say. But the official channels all suggest no.

You'll never really know I suppose, but it's so much easier to say "Oh my God, bodies in the basement!" and see how that could spread and morph and become something sinister and mysterious. Basements are underground and we do love questioning what happens in the bowels of the Earth as some mysterious netherworld. Literally, our fascination with the underworld is manifesting here.

It's very apparent that Robert Joe is a firm skeptic—a stance for which I have the utmost respect—and that he does not believe in ghosts...at least, not *literally*. During our interview, I was intrigued to discover that he does not think that the ghost stories surrounding Clark have a paranormal explanation, instead finding it more likely to be attributable to cultural factors.

To be honest, I think every culture all over the world has superstitious beliefs...in the west, they might be often couched in language that makes them sound more religious. I don't differentiate between ghost stories, religious stories, cultural superstitions—they're all part of a cultural fabric that makes up each society and they're all unique in their own way. I tend to find that when you get to the "old world" cultures, such as Europe, Asia, etc., those older traditions and beliefs manage to stay alive more vividly than say in the west, i.e., the U.S.

But then again, there was more or less a genocide of the old world culture there so of course those traditions are lost.

European and Judeo Christian beliefs still run rampant in the more established older societies of New England and down South. The TV show *X-Files* had great fun exploring those stories as a sort of American Gothic tradition.

So in the Phillippines, yes, I think the Filipinos, being influenced from a mix of old world Spanish culture, traditional Filipino culture, are somewhat pre-disposed to these beliefs. In fact, I'd say overall Asia is more predisposed to these beliefs than say North America or the "New World." That's why our show is based in Asia, lots of rich stories to explore.

Grabbing a flashlight and camera, Robert wasted no time and headed down to the basement to check things out—alone. All due credit must be given to the man for his courage, because the basement of the old Clark hospital is not a pleasant place in which to spend the night. Vandals have broken in numerous times and left most of the surfaces scarred with graffiti, some of it rather threatening and sinister in nature. The place *looks* like it ought to be haunted, whether it actually is or is not. Plenty of animals have created their nests down there and have set up homes for the duration.

"It felt very uncomfortable," Robert confirmed. "It was late at night, in a dank basement full of cockroaches and bats and who knows what else. So the atmosphere was quite suffocating. Mostly a combination of dust and feces, I imagine."

Robert also went on to explore what was once the hospital's mental health ward, noting that there was an odd feeling about the place—that something "felt off" about it—and I asked him to describe his impressions in a little more detail.

Yeah, that mental ward was *great*...it was so creepy and overgrown and there were clear signs of war gamers that had been through the space, telltale plastic BB gun pellets everywhere. That, combined with the rundown nature of the place, and

American and Philippines Air Force fighters on the flight line at Clark Air Base, 1984. (TAKEN BY SSGT DANIEL C. PEREZ, USAF PUBLIC DOMAIN IMAGE.)

extra graffiti everywhere made it hard to separate the historic artifacts and evidence with what had been created by current generations of people coming through and crafting their own narratives with fake signs, spray paint, etc. So you could see that people had painted on signs like *morgue* or *operating room* (I forget the exact details), as part of their own ideas of what the space was and so it seemed very unreal.

Ghost stories centering upon this particular hospital are not restricted to the 21st century. Indeed, doors appearing to open of their own accord, disembodied voices, and ghostly apparitions bearing wounds and injuries were all talked about by some of the staff during the years when the Clark Air Base Hospital was still a working medical facility. It's difficult to legitimately visit the hospital today, and depending upon who you believe, this is either because of the number of violent and frightening paranormal incidents that have befallen unwary visitors inside, or because of the health and safety hazards of walking around a building that is basically falling apart. Security guards still patrol the area and have no hesitation about turning away the unauthorized visitor.

One organization that had no trouble in gaining authorized access is The Atlantic Paranormal Society (TAPS). In 2007, investigators from Sy-Fy's TV series *Ghost Hunters International* flew to Angeles City in order to conduct an overnight investigation of the old Clark Air Base Hospital. The reason given for their visit was that the security guards were too scared to enter the building due to disembodied voices and screams, the crying of babies, and the sighting of full-body apparitions. The show offers an interesting look inside the ramshackle old building.

Introduced to the same security guard who would later meet with Robert Joe, the ghost hunters are shown the exact same spot at which the guard claims to have encountered the faceless male apparition who requested a cigarette from him. A pair of hospital custodians then go on to recount the story of yet another faceless man who approached them while they were going about their duties on an appropriately dark and stormy night . . . at least, he appeared to be faceless at first glance. But when the pair got a good look at where his face should have been, they saw instead that he had only a skull visible.

Barely had the investigation started before the ghost hunters start to see mysterious flashes of light on the darkened walls and ceilings of the abandoned old building's basement. These lights would also show up on the crew's video recordings during their final debrief. Footsteps are then heard at the far end of an empty corridor, and when the team gamely goes down there to investigate the source, three knocks are heard, seemingly out of nowhere. The footsteps immediately cease. A line of graffiti scrawled on one of the walls, "Beware of ghosts!" suddenly seems like sound advice.

Elsewhere in the building, two other investigators are surprised by the sound of a disembodied whisper that seems to originate somewhere in the air between them both, followed by the sighting of a face in one of the darkened corners of the room. Needless to say, a search reveals nobody physical to be lurking in the area. This same visual manifestation—a face in the darkness—then appears to the *first* two investigators as well, shortly before one of them experiences the frightening sensation of his ear being grabbed by an unseen force of some kind.

Suddenly, there are noises all around the investigators in the basement—"like a whole troupe of people surrounding us!" as one of the ghost hunters puts it—a cacophony of noise, all of it from sources unknown. A white figure is fleetingly glimpsed, lurking behind one of the structural support pillars, before swiftly ducking back out of sight...in exactly the same location from which staff members have also reported seeing a ghostly white apparition.

Wrapping it all up, the ghost hunters reveal that they have successfully recorded what sounds very much like human screaming on their audio recording equipment, originating in a visibly empty corridor—just another twist in the fascinating tale that is the haunting of Clark Air Base Hospital. The TAPS team packed up their gear to head to another location on their world tour.

But what you saw on TV was only a part of what would turn out to be a much darker story.

I interviewed *Ghost Hunters International* star and TAPS team member Barry Fitzgerald regarding this episode of the show, wanting to hear his personal thoughts on the time he spent investigating at Clark. Barry is an intelligent and thoughtful man, and has obviously given a great deal of thought to what took place in the abandoned hospital building. He contacted me via Skype from his home in Ireland, and was very willing to shed an ominous new light on the events taking place within the abandoned old building.

"Unfortunately, we didn't have the opportunity to research the entire base and surrounding area. We focused purely on the hospital building itself. And the old Clark Air Base Hospital," Barry said thoughtfully, "is one of the few locations that I've said I *never* want to go back to. Not because of what was going on in the upper floors, but because of what I found down in its basement, in its lower levels."

This immediately intrigued me. A seasoned, highly regarded ghost hunter who considered a location to be so haunted that he would never step foot in there ever again—what had Barry and his fellow investigators unearthed down there?

"I remember that we headed down into the basement—I was with Dustin [Pari], and our cameraman was 'Snapper.' We were all moving with great caution. The hospital itself is an *exceptionally* dangerous building. It's a death trap." Barry wasn't kidding about the potential dangers. He and the *Ghost Hunters International* crew encountered gaping holes in the floors on all levels of the building, which led straight down into the depths of the basement. Groping blindly about in the dark, it would be far too easy for an unwitting team member to fall several stories to their death on the hard-packed floor below.

As if the potential for a lethal fall wasn't terrifying enough, Barry related that an anaconda had taken up residence in the disused elevator shaft, ready to greet any unwary visitor who might be foolish enough to open the lift doors. There had already been a close call when the team first made their way toward the hospital, as a snake had lunged at one of the directors while the group was tramping their way through the long grass. Fortunately, the director narrowly avoided being bitten.

The rooms and corridors leading to the basement were infested with bats. The *GHI* team made good use of a "bat detector." (Bats and some other animals make use of a technique called ultrasound echolocation, sending out waves on a specific frequency in order to help them navigate, and a bat detector is an ultrasonic device that interprets those waves and turns them into a sound that we humans can hear.) Making their way into the underground chamber, Barry and his colleagues were listening to the sounds made by the nesting bats. "We must have come across a few 'faulty' bats," he said ruefully. "Because every so often, one would smash into one of our chests and backs as we continued to make our way through their home territory, on the way the basement."

But as the investigators finally reached the basement, silence descended upon them. "Everything went absolutely quiet," Barry mused. "And I remember thinking, *now, what's going on here?* There was another hole that took us deeper again, into the real subterranean section, a huge hole that went down beneath the actual foundations. But my senses were screaming at me, saying *this is quite far enough.*"

Barry found what took place next to be very difficult to put into words, but he attempted to do so anyway. "Dustin and I started to try and communicate," Barry began slowly, searching for the best way to describe the experience. "*Something* . . . started to grow. That inner 'well' started to bubble up inside and said *Look, something's not right here.* And I have to tell you that before the footsteps started, before everything started falling apart, the only way I can describe this—and it really is the *only* way I can describe it—is that it was like *standing in a living hell.* The basement of Clark Air Force Base is a living hell, or at least it felt like it at that time."

I wanted to know what was causing such a strong feeling. "What was permitting that, I have no idea," Barry admitted. "I know for certain that it wasn't attributable to the things that we had on the upper floors, the communication with spirits that took place up there. That was *completely* different."

Barry and his *GHI* colleagues used a vice familiar to military personnel all over the world in order to try and communicate with any restless souls of the armed forces that might still haunt the old hospital—such as the faceless man who took a cigarette from the flabbergasted security guard.

"I found myself thinking, *what's the one thing these guys would respond to?*" Barry explained. "You must understand that to try and reach spirit, we have to try and find some common ground. I spoke to the crew and got them to hand over their cigarettes, and we used those to build that bridge over to those spirits. And when the cigarette was offered, we heard two different voices coming back. One said *I'll take that*, and it was followed by another telling us that it was too late..."

I steered the conversation back toward the basement. Barry let out a sigh before dropping his bombshell on me. "This . . . whatever it was...did not belong to the human realm. I can remember saying to Dustin and Snapper that we needed to get out of here, and quick. And that's when, all of a sudden, the footsteps started. Whatever happened in that place, it still lingers there today..." his voice trailed off.

After a pause to digest the implications of this revelation, I asked Barry whether he had ever experienced anything similar—or even remotely like this—on investigations elsewhere. "Not with *Ghost Hunters International*," he replied, "and very rarely elsewhere. I can't speak for my teammates, but that is why Clark Air Force Base is one of those few places that I will always leave well alone, could quite happily walk away from forever and say 'I'm done.'"

He continued, "There are times when we, as paranormal investigators, take that proverbial stick and poke that sleeping bear. Those are the times when we get bitten, when we should have left it well alone. And whatever's down there in the basement of the old Clark Hospital is ready to bite if somebody provokes it."

So what does Barry think is going on in the basement? Although many accounts of the hauntings at Clark Air Base seem to center around the ghosts of military personnel, whether dating back to the Vietnam era or before that to World War II, Barry holds the opinion that something much more sinister is at work below the crumbling old hospital.

"I believe this comes down to the island, to the very ground itself, rather than what had happened in the building. Something older, more primal...and something *much more powerful* is down there."

In other words, although Barry believes that much of the paranormal activity taking place aboveground at Clark can be explained by the more traditional type of haunting, he maintains that a non-human spirit of some sort—perhaps something more elemental in nature—is by far the bigger story, lurking just out of sight beneath the foundations of the former hospital.

"We've had our own fair share of dealing with this type of spirit activity around the world, not only in South Africa, but particularly here at home in Ireland. I certainly wasn't expecting to find it there at Clark."

Barry's memories of Clark Air Base aren't all bad. He remembers the local Go-Kart track fondly, describing it with great enthusiasm as being "potentially life threatening!" I decided to end our interview with a question to which I suspected I already knew the answer.

"So in closing, Barry, just how big a check would somebody have to write for you in order to get you back into that hospital basement?"

Barry's reply was both immediate and very, very firm. "I'm not interested. I really would prefer not to go back there again. Ever."

The wheel of history has since come full circle. Once again, United States Navy and Air Force planes are flying missions from Clark's runways—most recently, P-8 maritime surveillance patrol aircraft that are being used to keep a watchful eye on the activities of the Chinese Navy as it continues to build a show of force in the region. American Marines are conducting joint exercises with their Republic of the Philippines military allies.

Meanwhile, the former Clark Air Base Hospital continues to fall into further decay and ruin, hoarding its secrets and stories. Some of those I interviewed have called their time at Clark an almost perfect experience, with one serviceman going so far as to describe it like this: "It was unique. There was no place like it on earth. It was probably the most memorable assignment of most careers." Another told me most emphatically that it was "simply wonderful!"

And yet, others have told a darker tale, preferring to see the place as "a living hell." Perhaps both sides of the story are right, and the paranormal experiences that seem to plague the former hospital are dependent every bit as much upon the observer themselves as any other factor. For some, the base is idyllic and beautiful; for others, monstrous and evil.

All we can say for sure is that the closing chapter of the Clark Air Base Hospital story has not yet been written.

The Spencer State Hospital
West Virginia, USA

Also known as West Virginia's "Second Hospital for the Insane," the Spencer State Hospital accepted its first patients on July 18, 1893, and stayed open for the better part of a century. During that time, the hospital cared for arguably the most vulnerable and unfortunate members of society: the mentally ill and the developmentally disabled.

West Virginia state officials recognized the need for a second mental hospital in 1885 when the patient population in the primary facility reached an overflow of critical proportions. Patients were packed together like sardines in some areas, and something obviously needed to be done to alleviate the confined conditions. A site deemed suitable for a new facility was selected in Roane County in 1887, and the monolithic quarter-mile brick structure was soon under construction.

Roane County reporter and journalist Katherine A. Kean wrote a series of articles to mark the close of Spencer State Hospital in 1989. In one particular article, she stated:

> As one explores the hospital's past, a story unfolds of a hard-working, low-paid staff who cared for their patients as if they were members of their own families, even though they lacked the training and numbers to offer whatever actual therapy was mandated by each new trend in mental health over the years. A story emerges of the quest for humane treatment for victims of mental illness and retardation and those who fought to make this ideal a reality in West Virginia.[1]

Spencer State Hospital during its early years. Photo courtesy of West Virginia State Archives.

Kean goes on to cite the multitude of reasons for which patients were admitted (and sometimes *committed*) to Spencer State Hospital, as documented in the 1910 State Board of Control report, which include alcoholic excess, senility, hereditary insanity, worry, ill health, over work, head and other injuries, syphilis, epilepsy, paralysis, morphia, cocaine use, chorea, disease of the uterus, pneumonia, bereavement, typhoid fever, and tuberculosis and puerperal disorders (once called childbed fever).

But not all of those who resided at Spencer State were medically or mentally ill. As the facility expanded, it became something of a makeshift orphanage and geriatric nursing home, taking in children whose parents could no longer afford to raise them, along with the elderly or infirm who needed specialist care that their families were incapable of providing.

Due to the popularity of such TV shows as *American Horror Story: Asylum* and movies such as *One Flew Over The Cuckoo's Nest,* most people tend to shudder at the thought of what conditions inside 20th-century American mental institutions must have been like. And yet, the conditions inside the walls of Spencer State Hospital were more humane than one might think...at first. The images of patients being locked into tiny, cramped cells and strapped tightly into the confines of a strait-jacket are the staple of a thousand horror movies, but the reality was that patients were rarely locked into their rooms at all (in fact, many of the patient rooms had no doors), and during the first few decades of its existence, the hospital staff were by and large a caring body of people who wanted to provide their patients with the best possible care.

And then, the trouble began.

As the patient and resident population grew, the worsening economic situation was cited as an explanation for understaffing. Patient-to-care provider ratios of 8:1 or higher became the new norm, as the staff became increasingly swamped by a near-crippling workload.

The period immediately following the Second World War can hardly be described as the mental health profession's finest hour. Lobotomization—a barbaric attempt at brain surgery that would not have looked out of place being performed in a carpenter's shed or an abattoir—became the in-vogue treatment for what was deemed to be severe mental illness. Most mental health professionals at the time believed that severe mental illnesses were caused by disease in the brain, mostly the frontal and prefrontal lobes. Surgery upon these lobes, they reasoned, should alleviate the worst of the symptoms.

The earliest form of lobotomy to be practiced in the United States was a surgical procedure, performed in an operating theatre, which involved the neurosurgeon drilling a hole into the patient's skull in order to access the frontal lobes of the brain. Two doctors who specialized in the field of neurology, Dr. James Watts and Dr. Walter Freeman, pioneered a technique of accessing the brain by drilling in through the outer skull.

With the volume of reported cases of mental illness on the rise across the United States, the shortcomings of this procedure became clear: It had to be performed by skilled surgeons in a fully staffed operating theater. Freeman hit upon what he thought was a brilliant idea: the trans-orbital lobotomy (which soon earned the grisly nickname of "the ice pick lobotomy"). This was a brutal process of hammering a pointed metal tool into the patient's brain, by way of an entry point just above the patient's eyeball. The prongs of the tool were slid underneath the patient's upper eyelid, which the physician performing the procedure had flipped back, and then the tool (known as an *orbitoclast*) was hit repeatedly with a hammer until its tip penetrated the brain tissue, at which point the doctor would jiggle it around in order to complete the "operation."

The great benefit of this type of lobotomy, so Freeman claimed, was that it could be performed in asylums and mental institutions across the country without the need for an operating theater. Anesthesia was considered to be optional. The procedure was practiced extensively at Spencer State Hospital, sometimes by Freeman himself when he would drop in unannounced.

During the 1940s and 1950s, *thousands* of lobotomies were being performed in American mental institutions each year. There was little clinical justification for this procedure, and certainly no proven benefits. Some patients died during the lobotomy itself, others shortly afterward. Some took their own lives, whereas others simply wasted away or became violent due to the brain damage that occurred when the procedure was botched. What is certain is that the lobotomized individual was never the same afterward, and the change was rarely for the better. The lobotomy ultimately declined in popularity when drugs were released that combatted mental illness in a more effective way.

Not many hospitals can make the dubious claim of possessing a dungeon, but such was the nickname given to a makeshift morgue area located down in the basement. In his 2014 book *Inside Haunted Spencer State Hospital,* author George Dudding recounts a number of disturbing rumors that center upon this part of the building; for example, he attributes the sound of clanking chains heard in that particular area to the rumor that physically violent patients were restrained down there in the past, secured with lengths of chain.

It is an old truism that doctors bury their mistakes. This might explain the persistent story that doctors at Spencer State permitted the burial of the corpses of some deceased patients (those who had no family members to claim them) underneath the dungeon floor. Although Dudding doesn't buy into that particular rumor himself, he does contend that: "...to some it is believable because many floors of the rooms in the underground dungeon consisted of dirt in places, along with concrete in others. Those who frequented the underground areas beneath the structure have claimed that they could feel the ghosts of dead patients breathing on them."[2]

Dudding recounts a 1970s interview that he conducted with a Spencer State Hospital maintenance worker. The man claimed to have experienced multiple encounters with something (or some*one*) paranormal inside those walls, particularly down in the lower levels. His work was interrupted by peculiar noises, and more disturbingly, by something touching him when there appeared to be nobody else present in the room. Indeed, the man felt on more than one occasion that he was not alone in what appeared to be a completely empty part of the hospital. We have all experienced that particular sensation of being watched, and know just how unnerving it can be when we are all alone.

On a sad note, not long after he spoke with George Dudding about his paranormal experiences at Spence State, the maintenance worker took his own life. However, this the only employee-related death associated with the hospital. Another worker there, who is referred to only as "Mr. D.B.," told the author of his being harassed by unseen presences during his time there. Could that have been a factor in why the man one day chose to murder his wife? Dudding certainly believes that to be the case. "I sometimes think that some strange evil force from within the walls of the old lunatic asylum had driven him to commit such a heinous crime. Could it be possible that he should have been a patient rather than an employee at the Spencer State Hospital?"

Many of the former employees of the Spencer State Hospital have gone on record regarding their ghostly experiences at the facility. Reports of disembodied voices and other auditory phenomena occur again and again, including the wails and moans of those who sound as though they are in the clutches of pain, fear, and despair. Disembodied screaming has also been heard echoing throughout the empty corridors, a sound guaranteed to turn even the bravest paranormal investigator's blood to ice water.

Although paranormal activity has been reported throughout almost every area of the building, much of it seems to cluster in and around the lower floors and basement/dungeon. Eyewitness testimony regarding the basement bears a startling consistency: the feeling of being watched, or at least in the presence of some invisible entity.

Spencer State Hospital was demolished and replaced with a Wal-Mart, along with a bevy of other, smaller businesses—some of which still experience paranormal activity to this day, a legacy left over from the site's days hosting one of the world's most haunted hospitals.

Although the hospital facility itself is now gone, there is one sad remnant of those poor souls who lived their lives within its walls, before ultimately meeting their end there, without family to bury them. A short distance away from Route 36, on a hillside located close to the local Elementary School, stand the unmarked graves of hundreds of former Spencer State Hospital residents. These unfortunates had nobody to mark their passing, and therefore nobody willing to pay for a private funeral—some had simply outlived their own families, whereas others had been tragically abandoned and forgotten by families who were either unwilling or unable to care for them.

The only way that passers-by might know of their presence at all is a single sign, which reads:

Spencer State Hospital Cemetery

Spencer State Hospital, first called the Second Hospital for the Insane, opened July 18, 1893. Patients with many disorders lived in the facility, as well as elderly people and unwanted children. Many residents without families lived there most of their lives and are buried in unmarked graves. According to WPA information in 1940, Cemetery No. 1

had 750 unmarked graves, 7 marked. Cemetery No. 2 had 100 marked graves, none unmarked. Earliest stone dated 1902. Spencer State Hospital closed June 1989.

The cemetery itself is also reputedly haunted, which should come as no surprise when one considers its background. Apparitions have been seen to wander there by local residents. Could these be the spirits of Spencer State Hospital's abandoned and unremembered dead, still earthbound and attempting to draw attention to their plight?

CHAPTER 5

The Aradale Mental Hospital
(formerly the Ararat Lunatic Asylum)
Victoria, Australia

The next stop on our global tour of haunted hospitals and health-care institutions is in the land Down Under, as we make our way to the southeastern Australian state of Victoria. Named after a nearby hill upon which the early settlers conferred the name of Mount Ararat, the city of Ararat was built upon gold—more specifically, the gold rush of the late 1850s, which turned it from a relatively small town into a thriving, booming center of commerce. A major gold seam was found and worked by Chinese gold miners, which goes a long way toward explaining the significant role that the Chinese have played in the formation of Ararat's history and culture.

Situated on a prominent hilltop position with a commanding view of the surrounding landscape, the Ararat Lunatic Asylum was built to meet the increasing volume of mentally ill patients in the region, and first opened its doors in October of 1867. This hill was originally named Cemetery Hill by the citizens of Ararat, as it housed the local graveyard *and* the old Ararat Gaol (the idea was that potential criminals in the town below would have a perpetual reminder of what awaited them if they were caught, and perhaps be deterred from committing a crime in the first place). While it would be tempting to think that the hauntings in this area were due to a "they built this place on a burial ground" situation as in Steven Spielberg's *Poltergeist*, the truth is that the bodies were exhumed and moved to what is now the town cemetery prior to the asylum being built.

As the Australian public's perception toward mental illness became more sympathetic over time, facilities such as Ararat changed their titles (while continuing to perform the same function of safe-guarding and caring for the mentally ill).

The facility that began life as the Ararat Lunatic Asylum was required to change its name in 1905 when the Australian "Lunacy Act" mandated that all asylums would now be referred to as "hospitals for the insane." But just a few decades later in 1933, the newly passed Mental Hygiene Act took umbrage at the word *insane*—along with all of the negative connotations associated with the term—and so made it law that such asylums and hospitals for the insane were now to be labeled *Mental Hospitals* instead. In turn, the name "The Aradale Mental Hospital" was settled upon.[1]

Ararat was a sprawling complex of buildings when it was constructed, containing more than 60 discrete structures and having far more in common with a small town than with a healthcare institution. The designers had aimed for the original asylum facility to be as close to self-sufficient and self-contained as was reasonably

The flagpole at one of Australia's most haunted hospitals, Aradale. Photo courtesy of Marty Young.

possible, which is why Ararat possessed its own gardens, fruit orchards, vineyards, and a host of other sources of sustenance. It even has its own dedicated morgue, being something of a necessity for an institution that held more than a thousand patients and half that many staff members to look after them. Records show that at the height of its occupancy, the asylum was seeing an average of five deaths each week.

The asylum housed mentally ill patients ranging in severity from the relatively stable to the incurably insane. During the 19th century, it was not unheard of for some poor, unfortunate individuals to be committed to an institution such as Ararat for little more reason than having a series of seizures, or being born with developmental disorders such as Down syndrome. We can say with certainty that some, if not many, of the patients committed here throughout the years did not actually need to be institutionalized at all, but ended up in confinement simply due to bad fortune.

Indeed, the Ararat Lunatic Asylum was an extremely easy place to get into, and an almost impossible one to get out of once you were a patient. Leaving aside for a moment the tall and sturdy walls that enclosed the facility, rendering it extremely difficult to escape from physically, actually getting out of there in a legitimate manner required the signatures of no less than *eight* doctors and administrators. Two signatures to get in, eight to get out—that tells us a great deal about the philosophy upon which the asylum was run. Once you were in there, the likelihood was that you would stay there for a considerable amount of time.

Special measures had to be taken to isolate and safeguard those violent criminal offenders who were also diagnosed with mental illnesses, so the old Ararat Gaol building was converted into what was to be known as "J Ward"—a cross between a jail and a mental ward, which we would know today as a high-security institution for the criminally insane. In order to make the move from an ordinary prison to a cell on J Ward at Ararat, a prisoner had to be certified as clinically insane by a minimum of two doctors.

In practice, it was sometimes all too easy to get somebody confined to J Ward. Consider the case of Bill Wallace, who passed away within the walls of J Ward at the grand old age of 107, holding the record as the longest-lived (and longest-incarcerated) tenant. In 1925, Wallace was accused of being involved in a fight with another man over a cigarette, which supposedly ended in him killing the other man. The details of the case are murky, but what we do know is that Wallace was "detained at the pleasure of the governor" and, given neither trial nor conviction, was declared insane by two doctors and remanded to Aradale's J Ward, where he remained for the next 64 years.

J Ward was up and running in 1887, and continued to house some of the most desperate and violent criminal patients for more than a hundred years, until it was finally shut down in 1991. It is now a museum that draws crowds of curious tourists. The gaol was built to architecturally mimic London's famous Pentonville prison, which was heralded as the British capital's first modern correctional institution, and is still in use today.[2]

Both the old gaol and the ward that it later became would see more than a few deaths within its walls, such as George Fiddimont, the fourth governor of the gaol who collapsed and died of a massive heart attack in September 1886 while climbing an old stone staircase. In 2005, a local newspaper called the *Ararat Advertiser* published an article reporting that a visiting paranormal research team was fortunate enough to record the appearance of a mysterious mist climbing that very same staircase, which leads to the old kitchens.

There were also executions, at least three hangings during the 1870s and 1880s, before the gaol became J Ward—all of them as punishment for the crime of murder. A correspondent for Sydney's *Evening News* newspaper telegraphed an account of the hanging of convicted murderer Robert Francis Burns on September 25, 1883:

> Upjohn, the executioner, at once pinioned the prisoner's arms and placed the cap on his head. Burns was then led out on the scaffold. He walked with a firm step, and took his place on the scaffold. Upjohn appeared to be very nervous, and in adjusting the rope permitted the noose to bang loosely, with the knot close to Burns's chin. The hangman's attention was directed to the bungle, and he merely pulled the noose more tightly. Head warder Eankin then stepped up, pulled the noose more tightly, and placed the knot on the back of Burns's neck. Death was instantaneous, Burns's vertebrae being broken and the windpipe severed. The deceased left a written statement, thanking the gaoler for his considerate treatment.[3]

The bodies of all three executed men were buried within the borders of the Ararat Lunatic Asylum complex, where they still are to this day, interred in the standing position in unconsecrated ground, facing the old gaol walls, in the superstitious belief that their restless spirits would be prevented from leaving their final place of imprisonment. If you visit J Ward today, you can still see the memorial plaques dedicated to the memory of these condemned men mounted on the eastern wall of the exercise yard. Current Aradale lore holds that frost refuses to form upon the graves of the three dead men, which may say more about the local climate and the location of the plaques than anything ghostly!

The quality of medical and psychiatric care delivered there was, by the standards of modern day medicine, best described as rudimentary and ineffective, and in some cases verged upon the downright barbaric. Living conditions were poor, with some patients spending the entirety of their day naked within the confines of their room (or cell), forced by necessity to relieve themselves on the floor. The food ranged from bland and poor in quality to utterly terrible. Experimental treatments such as electro-convulsive ("shock therapy") and brain lobotomies would also have been the norm for some of the less controllable patients.

The Aradale Mental Hospital continued to care for patients until 1993 (J Ward had closed two years earlier) and some female patients were still housed there until 2001, when Aradale ceased to operate as a healthcare facility. Parts of the complex, such as J Ward, were kept open to serve as a museum. When stories of life within the walls of Ararat began to be told by volunteers and tour guides, the ghost stories were never far behind. Tour guides began to share, compare, and collect their stories, and it soon became apparent that far more was going on inside the old insane asylum than first met the eye.

One such story concerns a carved brick, which was kept on display upstairs, in a specific spot inside the recreation room. This particular brick was hurled most of the way across the empty rec room one day, causing an almighty crash to be heard as it landed on the floor. An increasing number of visitors reported the sensation of being touched, poked, or prodded when nobody else was within touching distance of them. The sounds of disembodied cries, footsteps, and voices became commonplace, as did sightings of dark shadow people and in contrast, the ghosts of the guards and nurses who watched over the former occupants.

On a balmy September night in 2007, investigators from the Melbourne-based paranormal research team *Ghost Research International* conducted their own investigation of the defunct Ararat Lunatic Asylum.

In a complex the size of Aradale, whose sprawling layout means that buildings are scattered over a wide area, some tough choices have to be made regarding the best place to concentrate both investigators and recording equipment.

"I think the biggest challenge of any investigation, but especially any at Aradale, is trying to have the access, equipment, and protocols in place to create an environment in which any event can be fully documented from multiple sources," says Darren, the point man on this particular investigation (he prefers to keep his surname private).

Based upon its long and colorful history, the *Ghost Research International* team wisely chose to concentrate the majority of their time, attention, and resources upon J Ward, once the old Ararat Gaol. Cameras were situated to cover the stairs and entrance to the old kitchen down on the basement level; the main cell block and the west wing on the ground floor; and the main cell block itself, up above on the second floor.

On May 25, 1872, gaol prisoner Thomas Wall successfully hanged himself in his cell on the second floor. The *Ghost Research International* investigators used this piece of historical fact to their advantage, placing a digital voice recorder in the same cell and leaving it running, in the hopes of perhaps recording his voice from beyond the grave. The DVR was left running for just short of four and a half hours. When the audio file was played back, it was almost entirely unremarkable—except for a 30-second period during which a whistling noise is clearly heard fading in and out.

The source of this whistling noise could not be satisfactorily explained—could it be the melancholy whistling of a former occupant of the cell block? It's tempting to attribute this whistling to one of the investigators or their guide, but all were present and accounted for at the time; they appear on the feeds from the other three cameras—so no human agency was responsible. Darren found this to be one of the most impressive pieces of evidence gathered during his investigation of the Aradale Mental Hospital. Referring to "the whistling recorded at 10:59 p.m., the source of which could not be ascertained" in an email to me, Darren went on to say that "DVR cameras at the time documented that there was nobody in the area. Although, when taken on its own, the event was labeled as inconclusive, it was considered worthy enough to warrant further examination of the area in any further investigation."

Ghost Research International sets a high bar for what constitutes possible evidence of the paranormal. Their post-investigation report throws out a number of light anomalies and orbs on the grounds that cannot be counted as evidence due to the likelihood of them being easily explained away by dust particles, insects, and other simple causes. One incident that appeared promising at first glance took place at the bottom of the kitchen steps, in almost the exact same spot that Governor Fiddimont died of a heart attack. A sudden flash of light inexplicably illuminated that lower part of the staircase, and was successfully recorded on the remote camera covering the basement.

Although there was some initial excitement concerning the light anomaly, the *G.R.I.* investigator that I spoke with about this incident was quick to downplay its significance. "There was a lack of corroborative evidence—with only the data being from a single frame of digital footage from the DVR, the nearby PIR showed no abnormality," he told me. "Again, the balance of probabilities would state that the cause was of a natural origin. Although rated as inclusive on initial evaluation, after a more recent look at it I would rate it as 'natural cause highly likely' given that it does appear consistent with a digital artifact and knowing that the camera concerned was a remote controlled motorized type." In short: not a ghost.

Although EMF meter readings remained normal, observers in the area would go on to report unusual smells as the night went on—one of which was the odor of soap, reported in the vicinity of the old bath house—and a feeling of such intense cold that it induced shivering in one of the team members, around whom temperature fluctuations were successfully recorded.

Shortly after 3 a.m., the investigators decided to conduct an exercise in provocation (although *G.R.I.* prefers the term "enticement"). A pendulum was used in an attempt to gain answers to questions that the investigators would ask. Several times, the pendulum did swing in apparent response. When one questioner requested that any spirits present try to make a noise, they were rewarded with a tapping sound that was not only heard by the investigative team, but was also successfully recorded—on no less than *three* separate occasions!

But perhaps the most sinister occurrence of the evening took place at the conclusion of a vigil, when all of the investigators had left the building for a break—with the exception of just one solitary researcher, who gamely volunteered to remain behind in a room that was close to the main control center. Very few people would be willing to spend even a couple of minutes alone in a haunted old building with the history of a place such as Aradale, so she most certainly did not lack for courage. But the intrepid investigator also had good reason to feel secure—she knew that she had lots of eyes watching out for her safety.

For those readers who are unfamiliar with the control center of a modern paranormal investigation, imagine a scaled-down version of mission control for a space launch. Banks of monitor screens display the video feeds from multiple live cameras, streaming in both the visible light spectrum and the infrared or thermal realms. In the case of the *G.R.I.* setup, six infrared cameras and two thermal cameras were set up to cover all of the area surrounding the control center. Even something as tiny as a passing mouse ought to be picked up on one of the cameras if it strayed into the area.

With the majority of the team exiting the building, all was quiet and peaceful. Then, her eyes drawn by movement, the female investigator slowly looked up. The closed door to the room was ever so slowly opening. Of course, it *had* to be one of her colleagues— perhaps they'd forgotten something and returned to pick it up.

But looking downward to the gap between the bottom of the door and the concrete floor, the investigator could see one long, uninterrupted glow of light shining underneath it. There were no shadows or indications of feet. Nobody was standing there.

The door continued to open and then slammed violently backward upon its hinges. The room outside it was completely empty.

Snatching up her two-way radio, the investigator put out a call for the rest of the team. The cavalry came quickly, converging upon her location from outside. They encountered nobody along the way in, and began to search. The building was empty.

Eager to review the footage from the array of eight cameras, the *G.R.I.* investigators started to play back the video files on the DVR. There were no cameras directly covering the door itself, though the surrounding rooms and corridors were heavily blanketed with coverage. Was somebody—a living prankster, say—sneaking around? Maybe there was even a wild animal on the loose (Aradale sees more than its fair share of possum activity)? If so, then their form *would* have been captured on video. But there was nothing, other than utter emptiness and silence.

What about a sudden draft or breeze? The windows were closed, and it was a relatively still and calm night. The *G.R.I.* investigators enthusiastically threw themselves into trying to replicate the phenomena, using their body weight to throw the door forcefully open. They were not able to accurately replicate the ear-splitting crash witnessed by the startled female investigator.

Lead investigator Darren later learned that this room had been the scene of many unusual experiences in the past when other groups had come in to investigate the building. Episodes of unexplainable nausea, sometimes accompanied by severe panic attics, were the norm in there.

When the exhausted *G.R.I.* team members packed up their kit and headed home just before daybreak, they had nearly 24 hours of video and audio data review, not to mention more than 1,100 photographs to wade through in search of anomalies. But their story doesn't quite end there. As the official *G.R.I.* report concludes:

> One of the team present at J Ward reported an event they had a few days afterward. While lying in bed they felt hands grabbing them. Upon trying to stop the hands there was nothing actually there to stop—the intensity of the touching only increased. There was a perception that this was an ex-prisoner of J Ward. In a panicked state they began to wonder if it was a dream, even though they now found themselves in the same situation they "dreamt," that of being in their own bed. The uneasiness continued for a few days afterward with persistent thoughts of how real this "dream" seemed.[4]

Although a totally subjective experience, we are forced to wonder whether this paranormal investigator was truly dreaming, or whether something—perhaps a remnant of a former inmate or prisoner—had followed him home uninvited from the Aradale Mental Hospital. I asked Ghost Research International team leader Darren what he made of the episode—was it simply a bad dream, an anxiety attack, or perhaps something else entirely?

"I personally would consider the most likely explanation of the event to be of a natural origin—'A natural reaction of the mind to unnatural stimuli'—as referenced in the report," Darren says reasonably. "Likewise, I would not call it a dream either—it may have been the mind's reaction to having thoughts of the recent Aradale visit whilst being a state in between sleep and being awake."

Although the Aradale campus has long had a reputation in the local area for being haunted, it gained far wider media attention when it was one of the featured investigation sites for the TV show *Haunting: Australia,* in which a team of paranormal enthusiasts, investigators, and an exorcist tried to uncover the mysteries contained within the walls of the old asylum. And the night chosen by the production crew for investigation just so happened to be the night of a full moon.

During the course of the show, Melbourne-based paranormal investigator William Tabone recounts his own terrifying experiences within the confines of the old asylum. Bill was scratched on the back of his head by an invisible assailant, leaving two long, straight abrasions, which actually drew blood.

The tech crew branch of the *Haunting: Australia* team introduced a diverse array of devices and technologies to their investigation at Aradale. One of these included a Tesla Coil, used to generate high-voltage electrical fields, which some researchers believe may assist spirits in manifesting in the material world. Use of a Tesla Coil is somewhat controversial and divisive among the paranormal research community. For example, the TV show *Ghost Mine* also went on to employ a Tesla Coil, after which one of the hosts of the show believed that she saw a dark black mass moving across the room. But on the other hand, during a seven-hour *Ghost Adventures Live* broadcast from the Trans-Allegheny Lunatic Asylum on the night before Halloween of 2009, a guest investigator attempted to use a Tesla Coil contained within a mobile plexi-glass cage to "trap and contain a ghost." In what instantly became the show's most controversial moment, the broadcast feed of this particular investigator supposedly getting an EMF meter yanked out of his hand by what he later claimed to be a poltergeist, looked suspiciously like he was simply throwing the EMF meter himself.[5] Would the Tesla Coil stir up a storm of ghostly activity for the *Haunting: Australia* team?

Those ghost hunters who have conducted investigations at Aradale regard the Men's Wing as being one of the most active areas, perhaps because it was used to house some of the most mentally disturbed individuals in the entire institution. In light of this, it made good sense to send one of the *Haunting: Australia* psychics into that particular part of the building, which had to be entered via a walkway that was nicknamed "The Suicide Bridge." (The second floor was the scene of a number of inmate suicides over the years.)

Sensing and hearing a large crowd of people on the opposite side of the entrance door, psychic Raylene Kable was hindered by the sensation of a male presence lurking behind her, tugging her backward every time she got close to that door. She sensed that this spirit was pacing up and down the corridor in front of her, and wanted to bar her from accessing the Men's Wing. Whoever this male spirit was, he was ultimately successful, causing Raylene to turn around and leave before she even went inside the second floor.

Not to be put off, a male psychic was sent to take her place. Former bare-knuckle boxer and psychic Ian Lawman seemed to be overcome with a nauseating stench upon entering the Men's Wing. Footage recorded on his mounted camera (and used in that particular episode) shows him struggling not to throw up, and also having a hard time drawing breath. Tour guides at Aradale tell similar stories of visitors and staff alike, who have suddenly felt extremely sick for no apparent reason while touring the complex. Some of them have even fainted, regaining consciousness a few seconds later completely puzzled as to the cause.

Lawman then got the shock of his life when the apparition of a female with electric blue eyes suddenly appeared in the diagonal viewing slit cut into one of the cell doors. Unnerved and startled, Lawman took to his heels and fled the area. "She was a psychopath who wanted to hurt me," Lawman would later say during an on-camera interview.

Nor was it to be his only encounter with the vengeful female ghost. Returning to the same location with a second paranormal investigaton in tow, the two men recorded the sound of a gasp or loud exhalation of breath from an unseen source. Going back downstairs, the apparition appeared to Lawman a second time, lurking behind the viewing slit of another cell doorway.

Tour guides have reported multiple ghost sightings concerning a female patient who apparently takes a delight in jumping out in front of visitors and scaring them half to death. Could this be the same spirit that ambushed Ian Lawman?

The eyewitness testimony of psychics can be fascinating, but doesn't constitute evidence unless it can be backed up by other, more tangible sources. The disembodied gasp captured on the second floor is a good example of objective supporting evidence. But more impressive still is what investigator Gaurav Tiwari captured on his full-spectrum camera in one of the deserted corridors.

Sandwiched between two empty and unremarkable photographs, the middle frame shows the distinctly humanoid form of a tall, black shadow figure, which seems to be staring ominously right back at the photographer. The figure is wearing a skirt or frock coat of some kind, judging from the way its silhouette is composed.

As evidence goes, this photograph is equally chilling and compelling. The *Haunting: Australia* team debates whether Gaurav may have captured the apparition of Nurse Carey, the most frequently-reported ghost at Aradale. Numerous visitors and investigators have encountered her restless spirit, prowling the corridors dressed in a pristine nurse's uniform. But unlike the sinister female spirit encountered by Ian Lawman earlier, Nurse Carey's motives are far more benign. Her presence is more comforting and soothing, as befits a member of the world's oldest healing profession.

This particular episode of *Haunting: Australia* is posted online at Youtube, and I encourage you to make up your own mind about the evidence that they have gathered.

For writer Marty Young, the first weekend in October of 2014 was set aside in his day planner for a creative retreat—an opportunity to explore the myths and legends surrounding the infamous Aradale Mental Hospital, guided and accompanied by a number of experts in the field of Australian paranormal research. Marty's specialist genre is that of horror and the macabre, and his fiction has been nominated for the prestigious Bram Stoker award. As founding President of the Australian Horror Writers Association, who better to unlock the mysteries of this haunted institution?

In his write-up of what would turn out to be a very eventful weekend indeed, Marty describes the everyday conditions endured by Aradale inmates (as related to him by a knowledgeable tour guide):

> Some of the things that have happened at Aradale in the past
> were truly horrific. An asylum was supposed to have been a
> place of comfort, but not even 100 years ago, our knowledge
> of mental health was in its infancy. We knew nothing, and
> unfortunately, it was only because of what happened at places
> like Aradale that we have the knowledge we do now. Even
> still, the list of atrocities goes on: leaving incontinent, severely

retarded patients naked in their cells where they would defecate wherever they wanted, only for them and their cells to be hosed down at the end of each day; surgical operations and human experimentation performed without anesthetic (while the next patients can hear it as they wait in the small cell connected to the operating room, and worse, watch it all through the peep hole in the door); rapes; an abortion chair that got regular use; day pens in which the patients were thrown every day, regardless of weather, where they would die of hypothermia or heat stroke; a morgue that wasn't fit for a pig, with heads left outside in the sun so the skin would dry and peel away, limbs tied to the branches of trees in order to drain; and lobotomies performed to "cure" patients of any and all afflictions (the youngest patient lobotomized was a 12 year old boy).

The Aradale tour guides had no shortage of spooky stories with which to chill their visiting guests. One such instance took place one evening as the guide was locking up cell doors prior to closing up the women's ward for the night. Suddenly, appearing as if out of nowhere, came the sound of running feet pounding along the floor of the corridor in which the incredulous tour guide stood. The footsteps were coming straight for him.

This particular corridor happened to be divided by a sturdy door. The footsteps abruptly ceased, only to be instantly replaced by the sounds of a violent hammering on the opposite side of that very same door. Could this have been the residual noises of a long-dead inmate, battering with fists and feet in a desperate attempt to break her way out to freedom?

Whatever it was, the tour guide told Marty and his group, was hitting the door with such brutal force that it was making the wall shake. Displaying considerably greater bravery than most people would in such a situation, the guide opened the door and peeked around it...the corridor was completely and utterly empty.

A friend of Marty's visited Aradale and showed him a photograph he had taken of one of the windows while he was there. The photo appears to be quite unremarkable at first glance, until one looks closer and notices that a face seems to be peering out from behind the glass. That stairwell happens to have been blocked off, completely inaccessible these days...and yet, the face is quite distinctly there.

Intrigued by stories such as this (but retaining an attitude of healthy skepticism) Marty continued on his tour of the sprawling medical complex. But it wasn't to be long before strange things started to take place. The ghostly inhabitants of Aradale would soon turn out to be anything but shy.

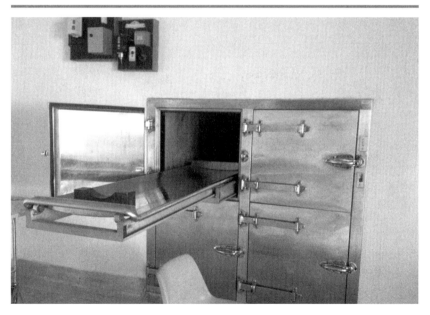

Sliding body drawers at Aradale. PHOTO COURTESY OF MARTY YOUNG.

During two nights of that same weekend, the Australian Paranormal Research Society conducted a scientific investigation into the paranormal aspects of the hospital and Marty was fortunate enough to be permitted to join them—not merely as an observer, but as an active participant.

One of the APR investigators was enjoying a quick smoke break, only to be interrupted by the figure of one of his colleagues, a female researcher who was beckoning him to come and join her in the men's ward. She was soon joined by her husband, who started to call out to the investigator, asking him to come across to the men's ward with them both. None of which would have been a big deal, except for one small detail: the investigator knew with certainty that both the female investigator and her husband were both actually located in the main hall, not the men's ward. Whoever—or *whatever*—it was that the investigator had witnessed, it could not have been either of them. Specters of the living (dopplegangers, for want of a better term) are not at all unheard of in the field of paranormal research, and although folklore tells us that if we meet our own doppleganger it means that we are going to die very soon, such apparitions are very rarely seen at the same time and in the same place as their flesh and blood counterpart.

Rounding up his colleagues, the paranormal investigator headed over to the men's ward, where they started to conduct EVP experiments. They began to receive abusive responses and threats from an entity that they nicknamed "The Beast," something which they had encountered in the past, and were firmly convinced was not human by any means.

The team was startled when their medium was grabbed in an invisible grip of some kind, and was unceremoniously yanked by the arm into one of the cell doorways. Reacting instantly, the medium threw out his arms and grabbed the door frame, anchoring himself there with a firm grip so that he could not be pulled all the way into the cell. The entire incident was captured on video, and although Marty did not witness the incident himself, he *has* seen the footage, which appears to have made up his mind about its validity. His scientific brain (as opposed to, say, the emotional or creative part of it) has the following comment:

"I have seen this film. It's quite something."

"Scientist Brain Comment: Could he have grown dizzy and lost his balance, stumbling in a way that made it look like he was pulled towards the cell?

"Unlikely, as those with him, who saw it happen, said it was as if someone (or something) had grabbed and jerked him backward. The video seems to support this, too. I don't know Rick that well, as I didn't really get the chance to speak to him, but he struck me as a honest and open man, not a prankster who would do something like this. Rick, Bill, and the rest of the APS take what they do far too seriously for any kind of carry-on like this."

"So, that whole episode was very weird, and hard to explain in any simple way. Visual manifestations, audio experiences, and physical violence."

As the night wore on, the APS investigators had shut themselves inside the men's ward in order to continue their experiments without interruption, so Marty and a pair of fellow writers named Chris and Tracy went to check out the women's ward instead. Chris took point, leading the way, with Tracy in the middle and Marty bringing up the rear, talking softly as they walked.

Suddenly they heard a voice say, "Ssshhh!"

Chris and Marty both spun to face Tracy. The voice had seemed to originate from her, from the position in the middle of their small group. But Tracy had not spoken at all, and she had not even *heard* the voice telling Marty to be quiet. Chris had heard it, and naturally thought that it was Tracy. So had Marty, and assumed exactly the same thing. Neither of them was right.

As midnight came and went, Marty and friends were still investigating the deserted hallways and cells. Hooking up with a group of four others, Marty finally got his chance to enter what many visitors to Aradale believe to be the epicenter of its paranormal activity: the terrifying men's ward. As the clock struck 2 a.m., the team made their way upstairs. Marty freely admits to being frightened.

> I was at the back of the group (again!), and part way through, could not shake the feeling that someone (or something?) was following us, walking right behind me, almost touching me. The others in our group felt uncomfortable, their skin prickling, and after a few minutes, I had to walk backward, keeping the torch shining behind be. It was utterly terrifying— I cannot express just how terrifying it was.

> Scientist brain comment: You are a wuss, easily freaked out, y'know. Too many horror movies, plus you read and write horror...

> Yes, true, and perhaps it was the result of the environment, plus hearing the encounters from earlier in the night that caused me to freak out, I don't know. All I know is how I felt, and it wasn't like anything I've felt before. I felt immensely uncomfortable.

> There have been times in the past where I've freaked myself out, but at those times, I will giggle almost uncontrollably, knowing I'm freaking myself out. At Aradale, there was no way in hell that I could giggle. I was more scared than I've been before.

Marty's story is a common one. Visitor after visitor to Aradale has reported the eerie sensation of being watched, sometimes breathed upon or physically touched, by some unseen presence. There is also the frequent sensation of being stalked, as if they were the prey for some invisible hunter. Feeling suddenly afraid (without an obvious reason to be) may be partly accounted for by the haunted reputation and spooky atmosphere of such a historic old place, but the experiences reported over and over again are much more intense than that, sometimes bordering on sheer, outright terror.

Undeterred by his fear, Marty returned to Aradale the following night for a second round of paranormal investigation. His group decided to take a more active approach this time, yelling out at the tops of their voices in an attempt to provoke a response from whoever or whatever might be haunting the place.

"Hello!" they each took turns to call out. "*Hello!* HELLO!"

Nothing but silence answered their calls. After a while of such fruitless attempts to incite a reply, the team quietly began to pick up their gear in readiness to move on. Then, the bell mounted next to the main door rang. It was a full and complete ring, lasting for one or two seconds, very deliberate in nature. It sounded as though somebody had quite distinctly and intentionally rung the bell, but when the team immediately went to check, nobody was there to have rung it. The area was completely deserted.

Breaking up into teams of four, the paranormal investigators dispersed to different parts of the building. Marty's team continued to try and provoke some kind of activity, while all the time measuring the surrounding environment with thermometers and EMF meters, and digital voice recorders were running continuously.

At one stage, my group was located on a stairwell, with me (again! C'mon, man...) near the top of the stairs and the rest of my group below me. We were asking questions ("Is anyone there?" "Make a noise if you can hear us." "Were you happy here?" "Were you a staff member?"), and then our EMF reader went crazy. Right then, I had the same feeling I'd had the night before, that something really unhappy, angry, evil, I don't know, was standing near me, just out of my sight. It freaked me out again, big time. I couldn't take my eyes off of the top of the stairs, knowing that the moment I did, something would rush down them and grab me. Or shove me.

A moment later, Rick the medium called out to us all, asking us to gather in one of the large nearby rooms. Going down the stairs, I had to walk backward again, terrified, absolutely fucking terrified, my skin crawling, my torch shining up the stairs, always up the stairs. Something was there, I knew that without doubt, and it was waiting for me to look away. When we got back into the big room, Rick told us that he had felt the presence of The Beast, the entity from the night before. It wasn't safe for us to be in small groups, we were told, because it was following us around, and it really wasn't a nice thing, very likely not even human.

On the stairs, the feeling that came over me was immediately terrifying, and exactly the same as the one I'd had the night before, walking through the upper level of the men's ward. And then for Rick to say the same entity they'd encountered the night before in the men's ward was here with us, that just freaked me out completely. It felt like the same thing.

Marty Young is a very rational, highly intelligent man. When he wrote to me of his experiences at Aradale during the writing of this book, I was impressed with his willingness to consider non-paranormal explanations for what befell him there. A lot of time has passed since he spent two terrifying nights there. Does he now believe that what happened to him can be written off as a combination of an active imagination, nervousness, and an environment geared toward triggering them both?

I've been seriously scared before (caught in the Canberra bushfires, involved in serious accidents, waiting to jump out of an aeroplane with a parachute, etc.), but what I experienced at Aradale was something else entirely. I am an open-minded sceptic who requires conclusive proof to believe in something. My personal feeling is that the majority of hauntings, including those reported from Aradale, have a much more natural, scientific explanation.

And yet, in the cold light of day, even now so many months removed from my experience, I cannot shake the belief that there was something following me along those dark and silent hallways of the men's ward that night, just waiting for me to look away. What that thing was, I have no idea, but I cannot recall ever being as terrified as I was then.

I'll admit after everything that had happened beforehand, I was excited and desperate to witness something supernatural myself, something I could not explain away via science. I was also feeling a bit let down and that made me bold, brave, crazy. I was ready to saunter through the men's ward alone, yawning at the creaks and groans of the old place, and scoffing at the tales of others. That didn't happen; I ended up with a small group of others, and as we walked through that old building, the sensation that something was at first watching us from a distance, and then creeping up closer and closer until it was following along right behind us, it was a feeling impossible to ignore. Some huge terrifying presence behind me that forced me to walk backward, my torchlight exposing all the shadows I could, my breathing fast, almost hyperventilating, because I knew by then that the moment I stopped looking, it would come for me, and get me. The others with me were also very uncomfortable, and we all decided we'd had enough and wanted out of there, so we got out of there.

It still amazes me, that feeling. I've tried to put it down to setting, historical knowledge, my reasons for being there that weekend, etc., but I just can't. I can't shrug it off so easily. This is even more annoying because it's not the conclusive proof I wanted, and trying to convey to those who weren't there just how frightening it was doesn't do the experience justice. I wonder if that's the nature of supernatural experiences.

Marty is determined to go back, feeling that his first trip to Aradale raised more questions than it did answers. He would like to go in a smaller group next time. Twenty-plus investigators, he points out, detracted from the atmosphere a little.

And what of Aradale today? The complex still stands, and parts of it can be visited by the public during organized tours, particularly of the notorious J Ward. Student vintners are taught how to make wine at a trade school and college located on the same campus, watched over by the ghosts of Aradale patients and staff members alike.

"Could Aradale Lunatic Asylum be haunted?" Marty Young asks himself rhetorically. "My scientist brain says that it very well could be..."

The Linda Vista Community Hospital
Los Angeles, California, USA

With lights flashing and sirens blaring, an ambulance screeches to a halt outside a busy downtown Chicago hospital. Yanking the rear doors open, the paramedic crew desperately wheels out a critically ill drug overdose patient on the gurney. Snapping out vital signs and an arrival report in terse voices, the paramedics propel their patient through bleak hospital corridors lit by strip lights. Gurney wheels squeaking on the tile floor, the medics finally slam through a set of double doors into the resuscitation room, transferring her into the hands of the waiting resuscitation team.

Although this happens on a daily basis in the real emergency rooms of the bigger Chicago hospitals, this particular overdose was staged for the cameras many miles away from the Windy City. It is actually a scene from the pilot episode of the award-winning TV hospital drama *E.R.,* which was based upon the medical residency experiences of the late author Michael Crichton. It was filmed within the walls of one of the world's most haunted hospitals, the Linda Vista Community Hospital. Whether or not you've ever stepped foot in the Los Angeles neighborhood of Boyle Heights, it is very likely that you've seen the Linda Vista Community Hospital before, either on the silver screen or on TV.

The supernatural adventures of *Buffy the Vampire Slayer;* the macabre life of serial killer and blood splatter analyst *Dexter;* the vampires of *True Blood* (whose production crew filmed a pack of real wolves running through the lobby); Clint Eastwood's Secret Service Agent hunting presidential assassin John Malkovich during *In the Line of Fire;* Dustin Hoffman's virus-hunting doctor in *Outbreak;* Arnold Schwarzenegger's cop in *End of Days;* and the military heroes of Michael Bay's *Pearl Harbor* were all filmed on location at this run-down old Los Angeles hospital, long-abandoned and redressed as countless movie and TV production sets. And as if it could possibly get any cooler than that, Duran Duran and Alice Cooper have both filmed music videos there, along with a score of other bands during the past 30 years.

The hospital can trace its origins back to the Santa Fe Railroad. At the dawn of the 20th century, there was a very real need for the railroad workers to receive affordable and accessible health care. Railroad work carried its own unique set of dangers and medical hazards, so business at the newly built Santa Fe Coastlines Hospital was brisk, and the hospital saw rapid growth. But times must ultimately change, and neighborhoods tend to as well. The area surrounding the railroad hospital slowly became poorer, and therefore the patients less capable of paying their bills, forcing the reluctant hospital administrators to make financial cutbacks.

Where one finds poverty, one also tends to find violence. The Linda Vista Community Hospital, as it soon came to be known,

Linda Vista Hospital. Photo courtesy of Wikimedia Commons user Los _ Angeles.

soon found itself becoming what those in the emergency medical services like to call a "knife and gun club"; the sort of facility that sees a high volume of violent trauma patients. Victims of shootings, stabbings, and other violent crimes became the new norm as the city of Los Angeles was caught in the grip of a bloody gang war. One doctor, who tried unsuccessfully to save the life of a gang member who had been shot, was then shot dead himself by the victim's fellow gang members in the parking lot outside Linda Vista. His ghost now haunts the hospital, having been seen by night security guards and visiting ghost hunters alike.

This tide of violence reached such a peak during the 1980s that Linda Vista was forced to close down its emergency room to ambulances. Death rates inside the hospital had risen steadily, which was blamed by some on the equally steady decrease in funding that resulted from the large volume of patients who just couldn't afford to pay their medical bills. But dark rumors also began to circulate of exhausted, overworked, and sometimes just plain incompetent staff members performing substandard patient care, which also contributed to the rising mortality rates.

Like so many of its trauma patients, Linda Vista Community Hospital basically bled to death. The more skilled among the medical staff slowly drifted away to take jobs in facilities that were better-funded, and therefore also paid better. The hospital doors were closed to real patients for the last time in 1991. And it was then that the ghost stories started to circulate.

The shrill cries of a distressed young girl have been heard by passers-by, originating from somewhere on the lower floors (she is most frequently reported on the first floor)—and she is also heard humming and singing from time to time. A mysterious green light has also been witnessed, shining from inside the darkened and deserted rooms after nightfall. As the hospital became a big draw for ghost-hunting teams, stories abounded of investigators hearing voices and seeing shadow figures and unexplained lights inside the building, with some even getting pushed and shoved by unseen forces.

Marcus Lindsey and Clare Benavides, co-founders of the research team *Paranormal EXP* conducted their own investigation at the Linda Vista Community Hospital in November of 2010. Although they had visited the ramshackle old place the year before, they had done little more than explore the nooks and crannies on that first occasion. This time, however, they planned to investigate in earnest. Beginning their vigil up on the third floor of the long-abandoned building, Marcus and Clare were almost immediately surprised by a loud bang that seemed to originate in the wall somewhere behind them in the hallway.

"We attempted to locate the source but we were unable to," Marcus says. "We didn't hear anything similar on any other investigation at Linda Vista." They never did figure out what caused the bang.

When I interviewed Marcus for this book, I asked him what it felt like to walk the corridors of Linda Vista. He told me the following: "Honestly, during our first visit to Linda Vista, the place felt very intimidating and it made us feel very uneasy," Marcus told me. "Our minds played tricks on our eyes and definitely deceived us. But, once you get a feel for the place and know the layout of such a humongous location, you start to feel much more relaxed in the environment. Even after our initial visit, you still can't help but feel like you're not alone there."

Audio phenomena continued to follow the team, including the measured tread of footsteps along the corridor, which were heard when Lindsey and Benavides were standing quietly at the third floor nurses' station. Displaying a level of bravery that many people would find difficult to summon, the two investigators advanced in the direction of the footsteps, probing the darkness with their flashlight beams...only to have the footsteps stop when they approached, leaving nothing more than a dark and empty corridor filled with more questions than answers.

Lindsey and Benavides also captured a number of EVP recordings, some of which were clearer than others. "*I'm in here,*" one declared, while another responded to a question with a rather more sinister statement, "*Been watching you....*

Coincidence—it may be more accurate to say *apparent* coincidence—plagues the field of paranormal investigation. To give one personal example: one night, when I was attending a charity investigation at a historic mansion in Denver, Colorado, a small group of people were conducting experiments with a "Spirit Box." For those who may not be familiar with this device, (known also as "Frank's Box" in deference to its creator, Frank Sumption) it generates words from a computer database, based upon energy levels in the surrounding environment, and speaks to them out loud in a rather spooky electronic voice. I was wandering around the lobby of this beautiful old house, chatting with various investigators and members of the public alike, and finally drifted over to the small cluster of people who were using the Spirit Box.

It immediately piped up with, *"Paramedic."*

I have to admit to being quite taken aback, happening to be a paramedic by profession. The experimenters seemed equally surprised, telling me that the readouts from the box had been largely meaningless up to that point in the evening. So for several hours the box had made little sense, right up until a paramedic steps within range.

As the old saying goes, even a stopped clock is right twice each day. But even so, a chill crawled up my spine at just how much of a coincidence this would have to be. I've seen the Spirit Box go on to make several other equally "coincidental" exclamations during my years chasing ghosts, such as the case in which a rabbit came up to the window of an old homestead that we were investigating and *"Rabbit"* was the immediate response from the box. My belief in the concept of coincidence has been sorely tested throughout the years.

The team from Paranormal EXP underwent a similar experience themselves, when they conducted EVP sessions down in the boiler room at Linda Vista. Next to their digital voice recording equipment, which was arranged on the cold concrete floor next to a couple of EMF meters, was an open bottle of water.

Marcus and Clare, accompanied by a male security guard, were the only living people present in the basement boiler room at the time. In fact, the security guard was the one who had suggested leaving an open bottle of water in the room, telling the paranormal investigators that for some inexplicable reason, this had led to some very positive results for experimenters in the past. Nothing ventured, nothing gained, they figured, placing the bottle on the ground.

Although nothing was heard by anybody present at the time, when that particular stretch of the digital sound file was played back over the speakers shortly afterward, what seemed to be an accented female voice could be clearly and distinctly heard to speak the word "*Water.*"[1]

The security guard was more than a little taken aback. When Marcus asked him what was wrong, he replied that the voice sounded eerily similar to a female voice that he had heard with his own ears on several occasions, speaking to him when he was all alone and patrolling the corridors and rooms within the old abandoned hospital.

Marcus considers this to be one of the two most impressive pieces of evidence captured by Paranormal EXP at Linda Vista, an accolade it shares with another EVP that the team had recorded down in the underground tunnel: "*Is somebody in here?*" This is the same tunnel in which, according to Marcus, other investigators managed to capture the apparition of a young girl on camera. The tunnel connects the body of the main hospital to that of the neighboring mental health ward.

The founders of Paranormal EXP were to return to Linda Vista in an unexpected capacity just a few months later when they were cast on the Travel Channel reality TV show *Paranormal Challenge*.

Why are some (I would say *many*) hospitals haunted, when others are not? All of them see their fair share of death, dying, and other strong emotions, not to mention violence and physical trauma if they have an emergency room. What is it about facilities such as Linda Vista that makes them become so paranormally active once all of the living patients have moved on? I put this question to Marcus during our interview. "The location has so much history and it's seen its fair share of death and despair stemming from patient abuse," Marcus answered. "So it wouldn't be a surprise that this location would have spirits attached to it. The culmination of traumatic events that have taken place there could possibly create a 'hotspot' of paranormal activity."

Marcus and his colleagues at Paranormal EXP would ultimately investigate the old Linda Vista Hospital some six times in total, and he is still fascinated with the place to this day. When I asked him whether he would like to go back one last time if the opportunity ever presented itself, his answer was unequivocal: "Absolutely!"

A 2012 *Los Angeles Times* article relates two apparently paranormal events that were experienced by long-term Linda Vista caretaker Francis Kortekaas.[2] The first involved a faucet, similar to the type that surgeons, nurses, and operating room technicians typically use to wash their hands while "scrubbing in" prior to surgery. These faucets are controlled by levers, which the person scrubbing in can bump with their knee or thigh in order to turn it off and on. One day, Kortekaas was walking toward a sink containing such a faucet when the water began to flow seemingly of its own volition and then

The rear entrance at Linda Vista. Photo courtesy of Wikimedia Commons user Downtowngal.

turned itself off again. The sounds of water flowing in empty rooms have been commonly reported at Linda Vista, particularly up on the fourth floor.

Kortekaas's second experience is one that I find a little more chilling. He felt a small hand—what he describes as feeling like his own daughter's hand, or that of some similarly small child—taking hold of his own hand. One is forced to wonder whether this is the spirit of the little girl who has been heard to cry out for help from the fifth floor.[3]

Since Linda Vista gained a measure of fame due to its reputation as one of Los Angeles' most haunted buildings, its frequent stints as a movie set (horror movies and TV shows were very common visitors) were interspersed with regular break-ins and acts of vandalism from an array of occultists, wannabe arsonists, and those who were simply seeking an encounter with the supernatural.

Another *Los Angeles Times* article reveals the apparition seen by a Hollywood Prop Master, who worked at Linda Vista for two months as part of a production crew. The Prop Master twice witnessed what may have been the apparition of a former hospital employee, clad in a white shirt, standing by one of the windows. A colleague of hers who happened to be walking past that same spot was suddenly overcome by the need to dash outside the building and throw up.[4] This may very well be the ghostly orderly that many people claim to have encountered, still making his rounds at the hospital long after the last patients have been discharged.

Zak Bagans and his *Ghost Adventures* crew visited the abandoned Linda Vista hospital during July of 2009 for the third season of their show, accompanied by fellow paranormal investigators Joe and Rebecca Mendoza. The Mendozas related their experiences of coming into contact with the spirit of a doctor inside the hospital, who Rebecca felt was aggressive and wanted to hurt her.

Poking around in the basement, Bagans seemed to be genuinely (and understandably) disturbed when he found ashes inside the grate of the crematorium, along with what may have been the remnants of a human tooth.

The *Ghost Adventures* investigation was an extremely active one. They had been inside the building for very little time at all before they found that a chair had somehow rolled itself out into the corridor, something that this particular chair had a history of doing before.

Auditory activity was also recorded several times. Investigator Aaron Goodwin heard what he believed was a disembodied voice telling him "*Ready or not, here I come....*" The sound of a male voice, the actual words indistinct and impossible to make out, was recorded in an empty corridor. Knocks and moans were picked up during the lights-out portion of their lockdown. What cameraman Nick Groff at first thought may be a growl sounded more like the Darth Vader-like breathing of a person on a ventilator when the footage is played back. And finally, the distant sound of a voice that cries "*Don't leave me!*" is haunting in every sense of the word.

Linda Vista had two trauma rooms—specialist emergency areas where teams of surgeons, nurses, and technicians fight to save the lives of critical patients who are bleeding to death, or otherwise dying from horrific traumatic injuries. As the *Ghost Adventures* crew lead was interviewing some fellow ghost hunters inside one of those trauma rooms, a bizarre humming noise followed after each question was asked, as though an unseen presence was attempting to answer on their behalf. This humming sound has been reported by a number of other paranormal investigators inside the same trauma bays.

It's impossible to cover a building with as much square footage as the average hospital using only human observers. Most paranormal research groups simply don't have the manpower to spare. As the *Ghost Adventures* crew is renowned for using very a very small team of investigators, it makes sense for them to supplement their head count with digital eyes and ears. Zak Bagans must have been very glad to have planted remote cameras throughout the hallways and rooms of Linda Vista, because they turned up some intriguing anomalies: a circular light anomaly, too big to be a dust particle, weaving its way down a deserted hallway, before finally disappearing in plain sight; and a white mist passing down the side wall of one corridor, which Bagans believes to be the form of a 6-foot-tall human figure.

Zak Bagans is well known for his attempts to bring about paranormal activity by provoking the spirits when on location. After splitting his team up in order to avoid intimidating any ghosts that may be present, he began to provoke in earnest. "Is this what you wanted—for us to split up? Come out and don't be scared! Come out and touch one of us, NOW!" At this point, his fellow investigator Aaron Goodwin gave a yell, and came flying down the corridor in a panic. He said that something had jumped behind him, and while it's unclear exactly what that was, a couple of odd sounds (one is a bang or thud of some kind) were picked up by his camera's microphone.

Sending cameraman Nick Groff into one of the surgical suites and trying to make contact with the spirit of the little girl who is said to haunt the area, Bagans and his team were stunned when they heard what sounds like the voice of a young child. But perhaps the more impressive noise went unheard at the time, showing up only on the playback of Nick's digital voice recorder: a genuinely creepy, breathy sigh, not heard by any investigators in the room. The breath is very distinct, and more than a little unnerving.

It was then Nick's turn to flee in panic, as he saw a female apparition standing right in front of him, no more than two feet away.

Another fascinating aspect of this sighting of an apparition is the technical malfunction that precedes it: Nick's video camera froze recording for exactly one second, the instant before the apparition appeared. Was this mere coincidence, or a physical side effect of a spirit manifestation? It may be tempting to write this off as a simple camera glitch, except for one startling piece of extra information: Aaron Goodwin's camera also froze at *exactly* the same time... for one second.

Groff narrates this encounter in much greater detail in his book, where he describes the brown-haired apparition as being completely solid, but with a face that glowed in the darkness.[5] The figure was dressed in a hospital gown, which implies that she was a patient rather than a member of the medical staff, and Nick estimated from her appearance that she dated back to the 1980s or 1990s, the final years of Linda Vista's lifetime as an actual working hospital...and the most turbulent.

Although we, the viewer, of this *Ghost Adventures* episode see Nick Groff leap away from his paranormal encounter after just a split second, he claims to have experienced a sensation of time being stretched out, feeling as though he and the woman made some kind of spiritual connection that lasted for more than a minute. The connection began when the pair's eyes met, which strongly implies that Nick was dealing with an intelligent haunting—something that was aware of his presence, capable of reacting to him and interacting with him—rather than a residual recording. Nor was the ghost simply standing there, mutely—she had one hand extended toward him, as though reaching out to him in desperation.

Afterward, Nick confessed to being absolutely terrified when this all took place. This fear is very apparent in the segment of the TV show that aired. Nick Groff's expression and demeanor all reflect somebody who has just sustained a massive shock, and he flatly refused to go back into the room again. One hour later, the closest that he was able to force himself to get was to stand just outside the surgical room, peeking into the dark interior. The sound of something being dragged across the floor caused him to flee, and he never did go back to that room again.

Groff is very frank about the aftermath of this sighting. The fact that he would see the woman's glowing face every time he closed his eyes for days after the incident speaks volumes about the intensity of this paranormal encounter, and Nick credits this as being the single experience that truly opened his mind to the reality of the paranormal. He even went so far as to pay a sketch artist to draw the ghostly woman for him. In a very real sense, she went on to haunt him for a long time afterward.

To cap it all off, a moment after the apparition was sighted and the three investigators calmed themselves down once again, all three heard the sound of a female voice saying, *"Thank you!"* The voice was successfully captured on a recording, and when considered in conjunction with the sighting and camera glitches, it makes for a fascinating piece of evidence.

Although the outer façade remains every bit as foreboding and distinctive as ever, the interior of Linda Vista appears to be a very different place today than it was just five years ago. It was purchased in 2011 by a private company that specializes in the development of affordable housing. Aided by a 9-million-dollar grant from the government, extensive reconstruction was carried out to convert the troubled old hospital facility into almost 100 individual apartments intended to house senior citizens. Lead, asbestos, and other potentially hazardous materials all had to be carefully removed before the structure became safe to live in once more. But so far as we know, nothing was done to remove the ghosts...

St. Thomas's Hospital
London, United Kingdom

Take a walk through the heart of London, past Westminster Abbey, and negotiate your way through the throngs of tourists that flock to the British capital city every single day of the year. Pass the Houses of Parliament on your right-hand side—do this on the hour and the resonant chimes of Big Ben will be heard from the giant clock that is towering high above your head—and cross the River Thames by strolling over the historic Westminster Bridge.

It may be worth your while to take a pause on the bridge itself for a few moments, because it has a reputation for being haunted that is now firmly entrenched in the folklore of London. Although the bridge only dates back to the 1860s—which is practically modern by the standards of a city that is so old—this particular spot on the River Thames has been a crossing point for most of the city's long life, going back for the best part of two millennia. In his book *Haunted Waters,* the great ghost hunter Elliott O'Donnell (one of the true pioneers of the ghost-hunting field) writes of Westminster Bridge that it, along with the nearby Waterloo Bridge:

> ...were well known to be haunted at times. Spectral figures were rumoured to be encountered on them in the dead of night and seen leaping from them into the Thames. Suicides from both those bridges were almost nightly occurrences in the early nineties, and more than once I narrowly missed witnessing them.[1]

O'Donnell also recounts a personal experience dating back to 1933, in which he was traveling along the River Thames from

Haunted Westminster Bridge, taken from outside St. Thomas's Hospital.
IMAGE COURTESY OF DR. ALISON LEARY.

Greenwich on a ferry boat, when he spotted the figure of a woman clothed entirely in black who appeared to have a veiled face. The boat was just approaching Westminster Bridge, when without any warning at all, the mysterious veiled woman turned, took a running jump, and leaped overboard into the icy cold river, disappearing without a trace below the surface.

Wasting no time in diving into the water after her, O'Donnell searched in vain for the woman, hoping against hope that she could be rescued from drowning. Finally, he was forced to conclude that the body had been swept into the depths, and accepted a helping hand back up into the ferry boat. The seasoned ghost hunter saw that the captain of the ferry was shaking his head sadly. The veiled lady had been seen on his boat before, the captain explained, and O'Donnell had no more chance of saving her than the last two men who had made the same rescue attempt—because she was the phantom of a young lady who had killed herself at that very spot, drowned in the dark waters beneath Westminster Bridge.

The passing of a phantom boat has also been witnessed at this stretch of the Thames, situated directly alongside our next haunted hospital destination. The boat is seen sailing quite normally underneath Westminster Bridge, appearing to be fully solid and real to the casual observer, but it fails to ever emerge again on the other side.

Londoners also like to tell of an anniversary-type ghost, an enigmatic man dressed very formally in top hat and tails, who has been reported to jump from Westminster Bridge into the dark waters below at the stroke of midnight on New Year's Eve. One is forced to take this particular piece of haunted history with a grain of salt, considering that most of the eyewitnesses are experiencing entirely different types of "spirits" as the New Year rolls around, but one popularly voiced explanation for this piece of folklore among Londoners is that it could be the ghost of Jack the Ripper, seeking to evade justice for one last time.

Westminster Bridge has not only seen more than its fair share of suicides throughout the years, as Elliott O'Donnell alluded to earlier in his writing, but it has also been the scene of multiple deaths caused by motor vehicle accidents, so it should come as no surprise to learn that this particular stretch of the Thames has been haunted for many years.

But now that we've taken in the air on Westminster Bridge and learned of its ghosts, it's time to cross that bridge and step into the Lambeth district of the city. On our left is the massive London Eye, the huge Ferris Wheel that dominates the Thames River's South Bank. But we are sticking to the opposite side of the street, where one of London's oldest hospitals looms large, perpetually gazing across the river at the Houses of Parliament—a place that has survived everything from the Black Death to Nazi bombs raining down by the Luftwaffe.

The original St. Thomas's Hospital is believed to date back as far as the 12th century. Historians aren't quite sure of the precise year in which it was built, but the hospital was named after Saint Thomas Becket, and Becket wasn't made a saint until 1173. (Becket was infamously hacked to death by four knights after getting on the bad side of King Henry II, who allegedly cried, "Will no one rid me of this turbulent priest?!") The first St. Thomas's Hospital was located in the Southwark district of the city, and took care of London's penniless and destitute masses, which it did until the 1860s when the powers that be decided to move St Thomas's to Lambeth. Her Majesty Queen Victoria personally laid the first stone of the current St. Thomas's Hospital herself in 1868, and the new facility was designed to be both bigger and far more modern that the former premises had been.

The 21st-century St. Thomas's Hospital is a bustling hive of activity, accommodating hundreds of in-patients and a multitude of other medical services. As part of the King's College London School of Medicine, St. Thomas's offers clinical experience and education to hundreds of new medical students each year. Operating on the cutting edge of modern medical care, technology, and teaching, this monolith of glass, plastic, and steel might seem like a strange place to encounter the spirits of the past. But if we have learned one thing so far in this book, it is that wherever there are the dead and dying, one also tends to find ghosts.

Many of the doctors, nurses, and other medical care providers who work on the wards at St. Thomas's have heard of the ghostly Grey Lady, who has haunted the hospital for at least the past hundred years, and quite possibly longer. She is described by those who encounter her as being in her early to mid-30s, and gains her name from the long-skirted grey nursing uniform of yesteryear that she wears, and is usually encountered in the area of Block 8 in the hospital's South Wing. It is interesting to note that nurses during the late 19th and early 20th centuries did indeed wear long grey dresses, until what we think of as the more traditional nursing uniform became commonplace after the First World War.

One of the world's greatest ever ghost hunters, the much-missed Peter Underwood, collected a significant amount of eyewitness testimony regarding the Grey Lady, much of it recorded and signed off by the doctors and nurses who have seen her in order to help ensure its validity.

In 1943, St. Thomas's had been hit by bombs dropped by the German Luftwaffe during an air raid. In the excellent *Haunted London,* Peter Underwood recounts the testimony of hospital employee Charles Bide, who was cleaning up some of the bomb damage on one of the upper floors in Block 8 when he noticed a figure standing behind him, reflected in the glass of a large mirror, which was one of the few left unbroken:

> She had a good head of hair, and her dress was old-fashioned and grey in color; it looked ruffled; and Charles Bide thought

to himself that she had probably being lying down, resting, after a busy night. As he looked at the figure, he suddenly felt very cold—although he had the distinct impression that she meant no harm—but the coldness grew rapidly, it became intense and penetrating, and Charles Bide felt frightened.[2]

Mr. Bide quite understandably fled the room, but according to his wife, he regretted this impulsive act for the rest of his life. Charles Bide became convinced that the ghostly lady in grey was trying to convey a message of some kind to him, a message that might offer some way to help free her from whatever torment she seemed to be suffering—and one for which he blew his only opportunity to receive.

There is one thing that many of the Grey Lady sightings appear to have in common: the sensation of sudden and intense cold, which often seems to accompany her presence. Time and time again throughout the years, it is described as an icy chill that seeps into the marrow of those who see this troubled spirit and are sometimes paralyzed in their tracks until she has either passed them by or disappeared into thin air.

Although she is sometimes seen to be standing still, the Grey Lady is just as likely to be seen in an apparent rush to get to some unknown destination. Her facial expression has been described as appearing troubled, as though some great emotional burden is being carried upon her shoulders. In one particularly intriguing episode that took place in 1929, two hospital administrators encountered her in between Blocks 7 and 8. One of the men experienced that common sensation of freezing and saw the apparition as plain as day, but his colleague saw nothing unusual whatsoever, being quite taken aback by his companion's aghast expression.

Unlike the wispy, transparent ghosts of fiction, the Grey Lady of St. Thomas's is sufficiently solid to be mistaken for a flesh-and-blood nurse—at least, until the retro nature of her uniform strikes the observer. Although making eye contact and interacting with some of those employees who see her, she rarely responds when spoken to—unless it is to a patient, in which case her demeanor changes entirely. Indeed, one especially fascinating aspect of the Grey Lady haunting is that she presents in a much calmer, far more tranquil manner when she encounters patients within the hospital, often standing at their foot of their bed during the long, lonely hours of the night, comforting and soothing away their fears, having lost none of the nurse's trademark compassion with the loss of her physical body.

Some in the medical profession believe that the appearance of a ghost on a hospital ward may presage the imminent death of a patient, a superstition that seems out of place in the modern world of high-tech medicine, but it seems to persist nonetheless. Although it would be impossible and perhaps almost useless to try and make this link in a large hospital such as St. Thomas, where patients quite naturally died on a daily basis, it is nonetheless thought-provoking to consider those cases in which the ghost was seen by a patient who was close to death and then subsequently died soon thereafter. After all, we know that the Grey Lady can be seen by some and not by others, as evidenced in the case of the two hospital administrators mentioned previously. We still do not know *why* it is that some people see ghosts when others do not (even when they are standing in the same room together), but it is undeniably true that those who are close to death report a much greater number of ghost sightings and paranormal experiences than those who are healthy.

Peter Underwood reveals several instances in which patients at St. Thomas's encountered the ghostly lady in grey, and then went on to die very shortly afterward. For one thirsty gentleman who happened to be suffering from terminal cancer, she kindly filled a glass of water during the night; when his *actual* flesh-and-blood nurse came along to do the same, he thanked her but declined, pointing her in the direction of the ghostly grey nurse who was still standing at the foot of his bed. One can only imagination the sweat breaking out upon the forehead of the living nurse as she turned slowly to face the end of the bed, only to find that nobody was standing there.

The Grey Lady graduated from serving water to that most British of institutions, serving up a cup of hot tea for another patient who received it gratefully from her one night. Still another patient made reference to a nurse who quite often came to tend him, a nurse who dressed much differently to the starched blues and whites of the other nurses at St. Thomas's. As you have probably already guessed, this particular nurse just happened to be wearing a long grey skirt. The Grey Lady was spotted by another cancer patient, apparently warming her hands by the fireplace on the ward. He died two days after seeing her.

The historic St. Thomas's Hospital. IMAGE COURTESY OF DR. ALISON LEARY.

A personal friend of mine, Dr. Alison Leary, spoke to me of her own encounter with the ghostly Grey Lady, which happened when she was a young doctor working at St. Thomas's:

I had worked at St Thomas's before becoming a student there so I was familiar with the hospital and its layout. I guess I was also familiar with the legends and stories but had never paid much attention to them. When I was younger we used to dare each other to ride the paternoster (a sort of open elevator) into the basement. It was supposed to be haunted.

In the early 1990s before hospitals had lots of retail outlets I had been on firm (a student with an assigned team) all day and all night. The only option to eat the not-very-appealing hospital food was between the hours of midnight and 2 a.m. The other option was to wait until 6 a.m. for breakfast. The only place to get food was the cafeteria in the South Wing of the hospital. This is the oldest part of St. Thomas's and is in the Italian pavilion style designed by Florence Nightingale. The South Wing corridor that connects the Nightingale wards of the South Wing is very long. The cafeteria, known as Shepherds Hall, was originally the Victorian nurses' dining room, was about two thirds of the way down this corridor. It was almost 2 a.m. and I was in a hurry not to miss "lunch." The corridor was deserted at that hour as I hurried from the more modern North Wing.

About halfway down the corridor I noticed her—a woman in a long grey dress with dark hair. In my tired state I didn't really process what I was seeing. She kept moving toward me—purposefully, very real, and not at all ethereal. Looking back, I heard no footsteps from her. It's very hard not to make any kind of noise in a hospital at night. It never occurred to me that this could be the Grey Lady. She came toward me and looked at me, before looking away and moving past me.

I remember the chill in the air as she did so. It was then that I recalled the stories I had heard of the Grey Lady—I turned to look behind me but she had already disappeared.

Many other people who worked in the hospital had heard of the Grey Lady—one of the common stories was that she warned of an impending death! Fortunately, I didn't hear of anybody dying on this particular occasion.

Theories, rumors, and legends abound as to the identity of this mysterious ghostly grey nurse. As such tales tend to do, they have grown in the telling as they are passed down through the decades, and each new generation of healthcare professional seems to add something new. Whether she is really the earthbound spirit of a nurse who committed suicide in the hospital, was killed on the premises in a fatal fall down an elevator shaft, or died due to a disease that she contracted while caring for the patients who were staying there, it is now impossible to say. All of these stories and more have made the rounds among the hospital personnel throughout the years, but one story fascinates and tantalizes above all others: Some of the St. Thomas's staff have professed their belief that the ghostly Grey Lady is none other than that most eminent of nurses, Florence Nightingale herself.

Florence Nightingale is a name that is both well-known and revered by nurses all around the world; indeed, many consider her to be the mother of the nursing profession as we know it today. But she is perhaps most famously known by the affectionate nickname of "the Lady with the Lamp," obtained in 1854 when she led a team of 38 volunteer nurses (having first trained them herself) and a group of nuns, out to tend to British soldiers who had been wounded in the Crimean War.

What Florence Nightingale and her sister nurses found when they arrived in Scutari was something akin to a nightmare. A small army of young men, with injuries ranging all the way up from minor fractures of the limbs to completely mangled and butchered bodies, were being essentially ignored by their superior officers; the wounded soldiers were rotting away (sometimes literally) out of sight in unsanitary and uncomfortable facilities, without access to adequate food, medical supplies, or treatment. The Nightingale nurses rolled up their sleeves and set about aggressively remedying the situation. When the army doctors had gone back to their beds for the night, Florence Nightingale and her solitary lamp were still to be seen, walking the wards throughout the long hours of darkness, administering medical care and emotional support to the sick and wounded without a care for personal comfort or rest. To the wounded men of the British Army, she was truly the closest thing to an angel walking this Earth that they could possibly conceive of.

Upon returning home to London from her service in the Crimen War, Florence wasted no time in establishing a formal school of nursing based out of St. Thomas's Hospital. There, young ladies were trained in the practical arts of clinical nursing, before moving on to practice their profession around the country. Nightingale wrote prodigiously on the subject of medicine and nursing, and heavily inspired the American nursing movement that sprung up during the Civil War.

Florence Nightingale died in her sleep in August of 1910, and so great was her standing among the nation that she was offered one of the greatest honors that can be bestowed upon a Briton: burial in Westminster Abbey, the resting place of Britain's great, good, and noble (located just five minutes' walk away from St. Thomas's). Her family declined this honor, choosing instead to bury Florence closer to home. The modern nursing profession owes an incalculable debt to this "Angel of Scutari," and the existence of this debt is acknowledged in many places throughout modern culture. For example, a U.S. Navy troop transport bore the name *USS Florence Nightingale*, the aircrafts used to ship wounded American soldiers home from

Vietnam were officially named "Nightingales," and many medical facilities around the world today bear her name.

But what are we to make of the theory that Florence Nightingale's restless spirit might be the Grey Lady of St. Thomas's Hospital?

Florence Nightingale was indeed dark-haired, and nurses of her era did sometimes wear the long grey dresses that the eyewitness reports describe. Perhaps more telling, the behavior of the Grey Lady—gliding through the hospital wards at night, bringing care and solace to those who are sick and lonely—would be in character for her. History also tells us that she was a woman who did not gladly suffer those whom she perceived to be less than competent or capable of meeting her high standards, which may explain some of the less tranquil encounters that some have had with her throughout the years. And it must also be noted that Florence Nightingale's ghost has been reported elsewhere: sitting on a pew in the St. Margaret of Antioch churchyard, located in the Hampshire village of Wellow, where she grew up as a young girl.

If the theory that intelligent ghosts return from death (or remain earthbound) sometimes because of a strong emotional attachment to a place has any basis in fact, it would seem quite reasonable that Florence Nightingale should return to the corridors of the building in which she created one of her greatest enduring legacies. And yet, Florence died at the grand old age of 90—and the Grey Lady is considerably younger in appearance than that. Unless we are fortunate enough to one day capture her on film, the mystery of her identity may never be solved.

CHAPTER 8

Poveglia Island
Venice, Italy

Nestled away in the crystal-clear blue waters of the Venice lagoon, sits the lush green island of Poveglia. Seventeen acres in size, Poveglia has that beautiful postcard look that makes you want to pull up a chair, pour a tall glass of something ice-cold, and sit down to take in the sunshine and the fresh air. At least, that's how it seems at first when you view the island from the air. That's before you take a closer look and realize that much of Poveglia's soil is actually composed of the ashes of cremated human corpses.

Although there are usually birds singing in the trees, the streets themselves are permanently deserted and completely devoid of all human life. There are animals aplenty to be found on Poveglia—lizards, rabbits, and plenty of insects—but there is nothing in the way of humanity...at least, nothing to do with the living.

The Venetian authorities prefer to keep the island closed to tourists and the public in general, and due to the island's association with the supernatural, even those residents who live nearby choose not to step foot on its shores. Go door-to-door in the locality, or ask around in the bars and restaurants, and you will soon find that those who live on Poveglia's doorstep are extremely reluctant to even discuss the place with outsiders. The most common piece of advice given to strangers is simple: "You're crazy if you step foot there." Poveglia has long had a fearsome reputation for being haunted, to such an extent that some of the local fishermen and pleasure boaters tend to give the place a very wide berth when sailing upon the lagoon, believing it to be a place that is both evil—and cursed.

Historians believe that Venice was founded sometime around the year 450 BC by refugees fleeing from the barbarian hordes of Attila the Hun. More than 100,000 piles were driven deep into the coastal mud and sand in order to provide the solid foundation upon which a magnificent city could be built. Famous for its bridges, canals, and the serenely drifting gondolas that are punted slowly along its waterways, Venice is also well known for such infamous figures as Casanova, supposedly irresistible to women and the world's greatest lover, who was born there in the year 1725.

The fortunes of Venice have always been intertwined with those of the sea, which soon became the city's life blood, mainly in the form of the cargo ships that constantly flowed across the Adriatic Sea bringing spices and silks from the Far East. The Venetians have always been seafarers, traders, and merchants by tradition and we need look no further than the great Marco Polo, who sailed from Venice to China during the Middle Ages in order to demonstrate that.

But the benefits of international sea trade brought with them one great and terrible risk: disease, particularly the bubonic plague, which was carried in the cargo holds of merchant ships by rats and fleas. The plague has decimated the population of Venice on several occasions throughout its long history, killing at least half of the city's inhabitants during the year 1348, when it sent an estimated 50,000 unfortunate victims to their graves.

During the late 1700s and throughout much of the 1800s, the island of Poveglia was pressed into service as a place of temporary quarantine for ships arriving from overseas that intended to dock at Venice. With the Black Death at its height, new arrivals would be kept in isolation for a period of at least 40 days. When a pair of ships brought the dreaded plague to Venice in the year 1793, the Venetian authorities responded quickly and decisively by not only quarantining those sailors who were infected to the shores of Poveglia, but also by shipping plague victims across from the mainland, along with the bodies of those who had already died of it.

In a sense, it was already too late—the streets were choked with the bodies of the newly dead, a huge source of potential infection themselves. The bodies ultimately got burned and interred, either on the mainland itself or on one of the outlying quarantine islands such as Poveglia. In scenes that must have been reminiscent of a horror movie, barges piled high with human corpses worked their way slowly through the streets of Venice, with fresh bodies being tossed onto their decks from each new intersection that they passed. These death boats then made for the open sea, sailing out to Poveglia, where their grim cargo was dumped unceremoniously ashore before the vessel set sail once again for another macabre round trip.

Those unfortunate plague sufferers who were sent to such an island typically remained there until they either returned to good health or until they died (in which case they were buried in one of the many rudimentary plague pits that were hastily dug around the island). So plentiful were the number of plague deaths that took place at Poveglia, local legend now says that the island was actually raised up from the charred ashes of those unfortunate victims.

The canal inlet at Poveglia. Photo courtesy of Wikimedia Commons user Chris 73.

Poveglia was not the only island used for the purpose of isolating the mainland from the horrors of the Black Death, however. The Venetians are now credited with inventing the concept of the *lazaret,* an island used to disinfect or quarantine those infectious agents that might otherwise have contaminated the mainland. Angel Island in the San Francisco bay performed the same function for the hundreds of thousands of immigrants flocking to the west coast of America.

An intriguing discovery came to light in 2009 when an archaeological team from the University of Florence unearthed a mass grave of plague victims when they were conducting an excavation on the Venetian island of Lazzaretto Nuovo (the "new lazaret"). What they found drew interest and attention from all around the world: the body of a *vampire.* At least, that's what the plague-era Venetians had firmly believed. A belief in vampires—the restless, unquiet dead, who were thought to crawl from their graves after the sun went down and suck upon the blood of the living—was commonplace. During this time of death on such a massive scale, hastily buried bodies were sometimes exhumed to be moved or to have other corpses buried in the same plague pit. The gravediggers were horrified to discover that some of these corpses had fingernails and hair that continued to grow after death, whereas others had become bloated when the rigor mortis faded away and the gases within the body began to expand. These same bodily gases would sometimes negotiate their way out of the corpse's mouth, which, to the superstitious eyes of the gravediggers, appeared to be a blood-curdling moan or cry. Speaking of blood, the tendency of some corpses to leak blood from their eyes and mouth only fed the superstitious belief in the vampire myth, which in turn led to the vampires drawing widespread blame for supposedly spreading disease, famine, and pestilence across the land.

The people of the time developed various methods for dealing with those who they believed were vampires. It was not unheard of for such corpses to be decapitated, with the head and body being buried at a crossroads, in the belief that if the vampire arose from its grave in unconsecrated ground, it would be confused and unable to find its way home to torment its fellow villagers. Thanks to Hollywood, we are more used to seeing vampires being staked through the heart in order to keep them confined to their grave for all eternity. But the people of plague-era Venice took the equally practical approach of jamming a brick in between the jaws of this particular suspected vampire, in the hopes of it being unable to suck any more blood.

Plague is not the only thing that has contributed to the haunting of Poveglia. During less enlightened times, the Venetian authorities used the waters off Poveglia to carry out the executions of convicted criminals, tying them up and submerging them beneath the waves until they drowned.

Poveglia has been occupied by various tenants, then abandoned, then reoccupied by others, over and over again during the past thousand years. In addition to its role as a place of quarantine and burial, the island has served not only as a defensive coastal fortress, but also an insane asylum during the 20th century. It was finally abandoned in the 1960s, and has essentially been left to decompose, like so many of the bodies of those plague victims who are interred within its haunted soil.

With a death toll that historians estimate at more than 100,000, it should come as no surprise to learn that Poveglia is regarded as one of the most haunted hospital facilities in the world. Locals have long reported the sound of piteous voices crying aloud at night on the deserted island. The mournful peal of a bell tolling, chiming out from within the old abandoned bell tower, sometimes cuts through the still night air. Ghostly lights may be glimpsed dancing among the trees. Legend has it that the apparition of a young girl, whose ghost stands alone on the shores of the lagoon, has been seen staring forlornly across the water at the home to which she can never return, hundreds of years after her death.

Poveglia is one of those haunted locations in which the fact and folklore are almost impossible to separate. The line between myth and reality has become so blurred that it is hard to tell just how much of the Poveglia haunting is grounded in reality, and how much is part of a shared tale that has been handed down orally from generation to generation, growing with each subsequent retelling until this undeniably beautiful little island has taken on a reputation far out of proportion to what actually takes place there. Precious little has been documented about the haunting, partly because Poveglia is so difficult to access legally, and partly because many of the ghostly legends contradict one another. Readers interested in delving even deeper into the Poveglia mythos would do well to read author Robin Saikia's thoughtful musings on the subject, including the video that he has made showing a complete circuit of the island's perimeter.[1]

The indistinct, shadowy apparitions of long-dead plague victims have been reported wandering through the burial fields and in and out of the ramshackle structures of Poveglia Island. These white-robed victims are sometimes attended to by the sinister-looking ghosts of doctors. These menacing apparitions wear the instantly recognizable beaked face mask that many physicians of that era wore in a blindly optimistic attempt to fend off the horrors of the plague. Wads of natural ingredients such as plants and flowers were stuffed deep down into the long, curved beak of these bird masks, in the hope that it would act as a crude filter against transmission of the Black Death.

Nor are all of the ghosts reputed to haunt the island necessarily human, as it was once used as a dumping ground for the abandonment of stray dogs. These animals, which would rapidly turn feral, had the run of the entire island, feeding on the smaller mammals such as rabbits, and sometimes, one assumes, feeding on each other, when they got hungry enough. Ghostly dogs have been sighted on Poveglia too, roaming freely through the fields and overgrown streets.

The island is split roughly into two halves, bisected by a narrow waterway that is passable only by a wooden footbridge. On one half of the island stands the buildings, long-neglected and crumbling; on the other, the burial fields where many the bodies of many thousands of plague victims were interred, and where they still lie to this day.

Among the few structures that remain standing upon the island today are the church, a boat house, the old lunatic asylum, small administrative structures, and what used to be residential quarters. Much of the paranormal activity seems to center upon the insane asylum and the bell tower, which has a particularly terrifying piece of ghost lore attached to it. Poveglia was repurposed as an insane asylum in 1922. Unsurprisingly, it wasn't long before the patients began to tell tales of ghostly plague victims haunting the institution. The nursing staff took these ghost stories with a huge grain of salt, considering that they came from people who were mentally ill.

The tale takes an even darker turn when the doctor who was tasked with overseeing the asylum was said to have taken it upon himself to experiment upon his charges, whether they wanted to or not. Horrific and brutal experimental surgeries took place, using a wide array of tools to open up the skulls of the unwitting mental patients as part of the doctor's quest to cure insanity.

If the local legend can be believed—and to this author, this particular ghostly tale reads like a piece of fiction, rather than the literal truth—the doctor was driven insane throughout the course of many years until he finally began to see the ghostly wretches for himself. Unable to withstand their pitiful crying and pleading for a moment longer, the doctor followed the beckoning spirits up to the very top of the bell tower, and in his madness hurled himself over the side. One version of the story tells us that the doctor fell to his death, but yet another variant states that a ghostly mist suddenly arose from the ground beneath his broken body and completely encircled the injured man's throat, slowly choking him to death. The deranged doctor's ghost has been reported in the vicinity of the bell tower, along with some of his erstwhile victims. While it is far more likely to be folklore than reality, the tale of the doctor's death does add a certain macabre capstone to the story of Poveglia Island.

Tracking down anybody who has actually conducted paranormal research upon the island has turned out to be next to impossible. Perhaps the closest we will get occurred when Zak Bagans and his *Ghost Adventures* crew spent a night there in 2009, filming an episode for their show. However, they were not permitted inside the old insane asylum due to its structural instability. Attempts to renovate the building began in the 1960s—in fact, it is still enmeshed in scaffolding to this day, abandoned by the workmen who fled the island after a few short months, for reasons that remain unclear to this day.

Wandering around the crumbling wreckage of these abandoned old buildings, both Bagans and his guide experienced some type of energy that gave them goosebumps and other odd sensations. This energy, whatever type it may be, is something that numerous visitors to the island have reported. Typically, these are folks who have avoided the maritime police patrols and snuck onto the island in an attempt to catch sight of its many ghosts. The grim, foreboding atmosphere on Poveglia usually incites them to leave fairly quickly ...some have even heard disembodied voices growling at them to leave, and never come back.

When calling out to the spirits of the island during their overnight investigation, Zak Bagans seems surprised to hear a voice call out an apparent response, the words of which he could not quite make out. Closing in on the source of the noise with tri-field EMF meters, the crew began to detect a rise in the electromagnetic energy fields—highly unusual in a building without any form of electrical power running through it. Further attempts by the *Ghost Adventures* crew to get a response from the island's restless spirits resulted in an impressive shout, which they not only heard at the time but also recorded on their microphones. Just seconds later, disembodied footsteps are heard creeping up on the group.

Shortly after inviting the spirits of Poveglia to "use our energy," an unidentified loud banging noise was accompanied by what investigator Aaron Goodwin described as "an energy burst" running through his body. It was never satisfactorily explained. Goodwin then began to feel extremely weak. Several light anomalies (looking distinctly different from the dust and ash particles that plague the entire island) were recorded, darting around the same corridors occupied by the team. As Goodwin continued to get weaker, feeling increasingly faint and dizzy, Nick Groff stated that he heard another

The central hospital building, complete with the haunted bell tower from which an abusive doctor is said to have fallen to his death, chased by the spirits of his former patients. Photo courtesy of Wikimedia Commons user Chris 73.

male voice in one of the deserted hallways. The electromagnetic energy levels continued to fluctuate.

It was then that Zak Bagans seemed to go berserk.

In what he describes as "an overwhelming feeling of anger and hatred," Bagans launched into a screaming, violent tirade directed squarely at Goodwin. When the episode aired on television, only a small part of this section was included due to the aggressive nature of Zak's behavior. Bagans claimed that he was temporarily possessed by something demonic, and that a "red filter" descended over his vision during the entire incident. He appears to be overwhelmed by the experience, and said afterward that he suffered a brief episode of memory loss toward the end of the event. "I remember screaming," Bagans intoned into the camera, "but I don't remember knowing what I was *saying*."

Leaving the building seemed to cure the symptoms almost immediately, although Bagans does subsequently take pains to point out that this is the first time the *Ghost Adventures* crew has ever had to stop an investigation part-way through due to a member becoming incapacitated. So concerned were they that the crew felt it necessary to break out a container of protective holy oil, which had been blessed by a priest beforehand. The crew anointed themselves with the oil and said a prayer, hoping that it would ward off any dark spirits that may have targeted them during the course of their stay on Poveglia.

After a short rest, the *Ghost Adventures* crew regrouped and headed out into the burial fields. While hacking their way through some of Poveglia's thickest vegetation, they smelled what Bagans believed to be the odor of burning. The implication is that it was perhaps a holdover from the cremation of so many burial pits on the island, although one is forced to wonder whether the power of suggestion (knowing the history associated with body-burning there) coupled with an entirely natural odor, did not simply combine and lead him to a false conclusion. Then the crew heard a loud yell from somewhere in front of them. More voices appeared to call out to them as they reached the burial fields, particularly after Zak donned a replica plague doctor's mask in the hopes of provoking a greater reaction from the resident spirits.

It would be entirely reasonable to explain the rustling noises heard in the surrounding grass as being some of the island's native wildlife. The same cannot be said, however, for the heavy footsteps that were heard approaching the team across the wooden canal bridge, immediately before something unseen knocked over their heavy, tripod-mounted light. The night-vision camera mounted in this area would later go on to capture what Bagans described as some kind of misty white shape, moving across the burial field to the accompaniment of unexplained voices.

Not to be put off by the avalanche of bizarre activity that seemed to be accompanying them, the three investigators upped the ante once again by deciding to split up and each go their own way.

Ducking into one of the long-deserted building ruins, Bagans attempted to provoke the spirits of executed murderers to talk to him, actually inviting them to attack him—and was rewarded with the capture of an extremely creepy gasping sound on his digital voice recorder. It is at this point that the footsteps returned, and a loud moan echoed through the abandoned corridors.

Aaron Goodwin chose the bell tower as his preferred destination, the death scene of the so-called "mad doctor." Struggling to speak with the spirits in makeshift Italian, Aaron soon gave up and switched back to his native English. Upon asking whether the spirit of the priest was present with him, a far-off howl and a loud thud greeted his inquiries.

Nick Groff took a different tack: offering medicine to anyone present who might be in need of it. His efforts were responded to with the sound of what may have been a male voice speaking indistinctly back at him. As Nick left the room to investigate, his static night-vision camera captured a dark shadowy form, moving across one of the pillars, accompanied by a low moan.

It would have been unreasonable to expect to conduct EVP sessions in Venice while speaking English, and to then receive answers in the English language, so the crew hired a local person to ask their EVP questions in Italian. Reviewing the digital evidence afterward from the comfort of an office suite, Zak Bagans and his colleagues then brought in a translator who was raised in the Poveglia region. He was able to verify that not only was the accent on one of those EVP responses very similar to that of the Poveglia regional dialect, but it appeared to be the voice of an old man, saying "Come here, come here." This had been in response to the question, "Have the doctors and nurses beaten you up?"

All in all, this turned out to be a dramatic investigation indeed for the *Ghost Adventures* crew. Some of their results are undeniably open to interpretation and non-paranormal explanations, but not all of them are so easily explained away. Considering that the island is not only physically isolated from the mainland by a body of water, but also that its fearsome reputation prevents the majority of local people from ever setting foot there (particularly at night) then it would have had to be a hardy prankster indeed to sneak onto the island past the police patrols for the sole purpose of causing mischief for a foreign television crew. While it's possible that the crew could have "created their own phenomena," no evidence of this has come to light, nor do I have any reason to question their integrity as paranormal investigators.

Throughout the years, the Italian government has tried to sell, loan, and, on a couple of occasions, simply give away their haunted island to various parties—never with any lasting success. One interested buyer hurriedly withdrew his offer when his daughter was violently struck in the face by a flying rock or stone, hurled with so much force that she required multiple stitches to close up the injury.

In 2014, the Italian Government auctioned the island of Poveglia off to the highest bidder. A 99-year lease on the island was ultimately sold to an Italian businessman for the incredibly cheap price of $704,000, in the face of stiff opposition from local residents who had attempted to crowdfund their own bid. One rumored use for the island is a possible site for a luxury hotel, an idea that has been floated more than once in the past by prospective buyers. In this case, it is easy to see why the locals might object so strenuously.

The message from Poveglia's spirits to the living seems to be very clear: *Leave us alone.*

The Rolling Hills Asylum
East Bethany, New York, USA

Rolling Hills Asylum was once the local county farm and poor house, a place that housed those who were unable to work or otherwise take care of themselves, such as the elderly, the infirm, the mentally ill, the homeless, the blind, orphaned children, and a wide range of other castaways from regular society. Opening its doors on New Year's Day of 1827, the poor house was basically one's last stop before hitting rock bottom. Where else might single mothers find themselves mixed in with the criminally insane? This was the place in which the mentally ill would go for basic shelter and rudimentary treatment. Those residents of the poor house who were physically able were set to work farming the nearby agricultural land, contributing toward the upkeep of their home and the rest of Genesee County.

For those who died in the poor house—although the precise number is unclear, educated estimates put the figure at around 170—there were rarely family members that were willing or able to provide a traditional Christian burial. The dead bodies were therefore buried in a nearby potter's field (the term for a pauper's graveyard), which was somewhere on the site. However, when the facility closed down the makeshift cemetery became overgrown, and its precise location has since been lost to posterity.

Rolling Hills became a nursing home during the 1950s, and played that role for a quarter of a century, then spent two more decades abandoned before becoming a shopping mall named the Rolling Hills Carriage Village during the 1990s. Today, it is in private hands.

Ghostly activity is plentiful at Rolling Hills even today, and it is hard not to find sympathy for some of the unfortunate souls that are said to haunt the place. One frightening but benevolent spirit is that of Roy, sent to the asylum as an inmate during childhood and remaining there for his entire life. A true "gentle giant" in life—quite literally, as Roy did actually have gigantism—his harmless but hulking shade is still seen, an estimated 7 feet in height, wandering the halls of Rolling Hills. His shadowy form has even been photographed.

Shadow figures are commonly seen throughout the building. The apparition of a goateed man is also a staple ghost sighting there, and with echoes of Harry Potter's "Moaning Myrtle," the ghost of an elderly lady haunts the ladies' toilets! Disembodied footsteps have been reported by witnesses who are exploring the second floor of the East Wing, coming from directly above them—slightly disconcerting, one would think, considering that there *is* no third floor above the East Wing...

Toys move around by themselves down in the basement, as though played with by the invisible hands of ghostly children. This

The Rolling Hills Asylum appears deceptively tranquil on a warm, sunny day.
Photo courtesy of Mike Cardinuto.

takes place in what is known as the "Christmas Room," because it is decked out with Christmas decorations. The orphaned children of the poor house once came there to meet Santa Claus during the holiday season, and perhaps they are the ones who are moving the rocking horse that still sits down there, or the ones who grasp the hands of unsuspecting visitors and give them the fright of their lives.

Some of the phantoms here are distinctly disturbing, such as that of a "Nurse Emmie," who asylum folklore insists was not only set on mistreating her patients, but was also keen to practice black magic at Rolling Hills during her lifetime. If there is truth to this aspect of the tale, one wonders what dark energies might have been stirred up during the course of those rituals.

The recreation room, in which inmates could escape for a while and perhaps even have a little fun, is known for having chairs that move all by themselves, and some visitors have captured the images of ghostly residents sitting on the chairs when they take photos of the seemingly empty room. Off to one side of the rec room is the chapel, in which objects also move without apparent cause.

One disturbing phenomenon that takes place in the boiler room has been reported by several visitors on multiple occasions: People walking down the stairs that lead into that particular room claim to have been pushed by some sort of invisible force. When investigators from The Atlantic Paranormal Society (TAPS) investigated Rolling Hills as part of their television show *Ghost Hunters,* star Jason Hawes was surprised when a door closed upon him while he was checking out a small room located adjacent to the boiler room. It would seem that whoever haunts this particular part of the asylum does not like company. The *Ghost Adventures* crew also experienced a door slamming violently at Rolling Hills during the recording of their TV show there. One wonders whether the spirits are becoming camera-shy....

Mike Cardinuto and his colleagues from Long Island Paranormal Investigators (L.I.P.I.) have visited Rolling Hills three times, and have worked hard to cover as much of the facility with cameras, microphones, and human investigators as possible. The asylum facility is huge, more than 65,000 feet in size—and that's not counting the tunnels underneath it, and the various minor buildings that surround it. It is down in the basement that the original morgue can be found.

During their research, Mike's team uncovered the story of bodies being placed in the meat freezers in the basement during tuberculosis outbreaks because the morgue was full to capacity...and not all of the patients were actually dead at the time they were placed on ice. No wonder then that the basement is so active. Coupled with the fact that electroshock therapy was carried out down there, we can begin to understand why so many EVPs are recorded by investigators in that area.

"One of the weirdest things we recorded there was down in the boiler room," Mike said. "We had a Geiger counter set up in there, and it actually started picking up some gamma radiation—that has almost *never* happened to us before on a paranormal investigation, it's so very rare. One theory is that a ghost manifesting might be emitting some radiation, which might have tripped our counter."

While strolling around the second floor of the East Wing, one member of the L.I.P.I. team was touched on the back of the neck in an otherwise empty corridor. The sound of disembodied footsteps and shuffling feet were a constant accompaniment to the investigators on this floor during the night time, and the rather less commons sounds of a doorknob turning and a key being dropped were also recorded. In the hallway one floor beneath, another investigator was setting up a remote camera when he was startled by the appearance of something incredible.

"He was setting up this camera on a tripod, and a shadow person walked right out in front of him," Mike told me during our interview. "He [the investigator] freaked out and ran down the hall."

When his fellow investigators asked what had sent him running, the breathless eyewitness told them about the shadow figure and then said, "I can't believe that just happened—stuff like this *isn't supposed to happen!*"

"He was one of the biggest skeptics in our group," Mike chuckled as he recounted the story to me, "and just that one experience made him a believer."

Investigating the Christmas Room, other investigators reported seeing a shapeless black mass briefly hovering in the air in front of them. This sighting was accompanied by a brief spike in electromagnetic energy levels, which quickly settled back to normal when the form disappeared.

Investigator Cheryl Wittmann was in the first floor restroom when the door suddenly closed on her, despite having remained wide open all through the night. Poking her head outside, she found the hallway to be completely deserted.

A ramp leads down from the East Wing's second floor to the basement. At 03:30 in the morning, investigator Thelma D'Amico was standing on that ramp when she happened to glance down and caught a startling sight in the doorway to the Christmas Room: a head and a pair of shoulders! Thelma and her colleagues knew that the basement was currently empty, but they searched it from top to bottom anyway. Unsurprisingly, nobody was found.

Of all the EVPs captured by the L.I.P.I. research team, perhaps the most fascinating—and disturbing—was recorded in the cafeteria, which also doubled as the temporary headquarters for the investigation. The sound of a chilling scream was recorded (though heard by nobody present at the time) followed just a few seconds later by a softer hiss. The source of these EVPs has never been satisfactorily explained, but L.I.P.I. are only one of many teams that have captured the screaming noises at Rolling Hills—indeed, the *Ghost Adventures* crew captured them during the recording of their lockdown.

"We'd already picked up an EVP in this HQ area that sounded like somebody had dropped a box and slid it across the floor, which was also pretty interesting," Mike remembered.

"The atmosphere in the HQ area is surprisingly normal. But once you get a little further inside…the third floor has by far the creepiest feeling. It's where you really feel like you're being oppressed. That's where the doctors' and nurses' quarters were.

"The second floor is what they call the 'shadow floor' and they had quite a few patient rooms. The atmosphere up there had its moments, at times it felt *really* heavy. We had a psychic in the group, and when he walked into one of the rooms, he felt such an extremely overwhelming feeling that he started crying, almost," Mike went on. "He was with another investigator, and they both experienced this huge temperature drop.

"The most activity we got was on the second floor," he summed up for me. "But the place where you feel the most *watched* . . . yeah, that would be up on the third."

Returning a year later for a second bout, the team experienced even more bizarre activity. Physical sensations included one investigator who felt that she was being "stopped" by something at the top of the stairs—something that she felt did not want her to be up there. Such feelings were widespread across the team, with a number of them feeling uneasy and dizzy, along with a definite lack of being welcome.

A set of legs blithely wandered past the doorway of the first floor smoking room, followed shortly afterward by an odd light being seen in the corridor outside. The investigator who observed this extraordinary sight would go on to report hearing music playing within that same room.

When Mike and two teammates staked out that same room, they heard the sound of a dog barking from a few rooms further down the hallway. Calling out to try and draw the dog—if a dog it actually *was*—toward them, investigator Cheryl Wittmann's voice was mimicked by something that called back to her in the same manner. Although the investigators heard this exchange with their own ears, it is fascinating to note that none of the responses to the team would appear on their digital voice recorders.

Many paranormal research teams now employ laser grids to help cover darkened hallways. These relatively cheap devices are used to shine a battery of laser beams down those hallways, creating a colorful grid when they hit a wall at the far end. When something breaks the grid, it is usually a sign that some form of shadow activity is in play. In the East Wing, second-floor beams were broken by something passing from left to right on two occasions. Needless to say, there was nobody else up on that floor with them at the time.

Down in the basement, investigator Peter Ferraro was in the middle of conducting an EVP session when an invisible hand grabbed his leg. This took place in the Christmas Room, so hopefully it was the hand of a playful child, rather than one of the asylum's less savory occupants, such as the spirit named Raymond, who researchers believe was a child molester during his lifetime.

"There was a lot of interaction," Mike recalled. "If you ask something to answer a question, you'll get a *bang* in response. We got a lot of banging there, and a lot of screaming. A lot of the activity is very intelligent, much more so than it is residual. We'd ask if anybody was in here with us, and we'd straight away get two bangs."

Does the Rolling Hills Asylum have any other mysteries for Mike and L.I.P.I. to unravel?

"I would just love to go back," he answers when prompted. "This is one of the most active places I've ever investigated. Every single time we've gone there, we've gotten evidence. In fact, we're going back there next year—and I can't wait."

University College Hospital
London, United Kingdom

When one considers its centuries of bloody and tragic history, it should not be the least bit surprising to learn that the city of London is home to more reported ghost sightings per square mile than any other city in the world. Accounts of shades and specters drifting through the halls of the many historic London buildings are commonplace; they are the ghosts of men and women who were both ordinary and extraordinary. Behind every ghost sighting can be found a fascinating human interest story, and none is more so than the tragic tale of a young lady by the name of Elizabeth Church.

As the 19th century drew to a close, Elizabeth ("Lizzie" to her friends and family) was a nurse working at University College Hospital on Gower Street in the Bloomsbury area of the city. Her fiancée was admitted to the hospital as a patient, and a tragic twist of fate found Lizzie assigned to care for him on one of the wards there. Although it's not known precisely what illness or malady afflicted her beau, it must have been something that caused a great deal of pain, because Lizzie was directed to administer morphine to him in order to provide some relief.

Morphine is a very potent analgesic drug that is still widely used today—in fact, I myself administer it to patients as an emergency paramedic. I may find myself injecting it into the vein of a patient who is suffering from a heart attack, another who has sustained severe burns, or to somebody who has fractured a bone or dislocated a joint. Morphine is a drug that must be given with caution, because if it is given too rapidly or in too great an amount, it may not only drop the blood pressure to dangerous levels, but can also depress the respiratory drive to such an extent that the patient stops breathing and dies.

For those of us who practice medicine in the 21st century, a drug is available to counteract a morphine overdose, so if the patient reacts badly to the drug, there is something we can do about it. But Naloxone (or Narcan, as it is more commonly known) was not invented until 1961, almost 70 years after poor Lizzie Church accidentally administered a fatal overdose of morphine to her intended husband. Unable to live with the guilt of killing the man she loved, Lizzie was overcome with grief and guilt, and the distraught nurse took her own life.

Doctors and nurses working at University College Hospital in the decades since then have sometimes been shocked to look up from their patients' bedside to see the apparition of a ghostly nurse hovering there in the background, staring balefully back at them. The apparition wears period clothing, and seems to be trying to convey a warning, one that all medical professionals would do well to heed: *Watch out for your drug dosing!*

Can it really be a coincidence that the mournful ghost of Lizzie Church is most often seen when a patient is just about to be injected with painkilling medications...especially morphine?

Curses are one of those things in which one either believes or one does not believe, and most of us today tend to laugh them off as mere fodder for scary movies. But for those who *do* believe in them, curses are no laughing matter. For more than 150 years, the framed portrait of an eminent surgeon by the name of Marcus Beck was prominently displayed high on a wall at University College Hospital. The nursing staff at the hospital firmly believed that the painting was cursed, and that any unwary person who should sit underneath the painting and then drift off to sleep would become seriously ill, and in some cases would never wake up again.

It wasn't long before a dark superstition grew to surround the painting: If the surgeon's portrait were left uncovered overnight, either a patient or somebody employed at or connected with the hospital would die suddenly because of it. Although most medical professionals are rational and scientific individuals by training and by nature, we are not entirely without our superstitious tendencies. The nurses at University College Hospital eventually developed expectations regarding the idea that Beck's painting had somehow become cursed. In what grew to become a long-term tradition, it was the solemn duty of the oncoming night shift nurses to cover up the painting when beginning their watch in the evening. Their daytime counterparts would uncover it first thing the following morning—until the year 2001, that is, when an opportunistic thief made off with the painting!

One is forced to wonder where the thief hung the painting. Hopefully not above any place that they might sit, or worse, fall asleep....

University College Hospital is also haunted by the ghost of a truly larger-than-life figure, that of the esteemed philosopher Jeremy Bentham. Among many other things, Bentham was a renowned social and legal reformer, who tried unsuccessfully to introduce a national prison that he intended to call "The Panopticon." The idea never gained any real traction, but Bentham was more successful in

University College Hospital, London. Photo courtesy of UCHL Arts and Heritage.

his efforts to father a bill that ultimately brought to life the Thames River police service, the band of maritime coppers that patrol the length of Britain's greatest river in pursuit of criminals.

Throughout the course of his lifetime, Jeremy Bentham wrote millions of words that spanned a wide variety of subject areas. He was an acknowledged expert in the legal domain, that of the natural sciences, and of philosophy in all its numerous forms. Most of his papers are preserved and archived at University College London to this day. Notoriously eccentric and prone to somewhat unusual turns of behavior (his future biographers concluded that he may well have possessed a form of Asperger's) this colorful character was well-known around University College London and its attached hospital for wearing distinctive white gloves and carrying a walking stick, each one of which had its own individual name. At the time of Bentham's death, his last walking stick went by the name of "Dapple."

Jeremy Bentham had a highly specific and unique (in fact some would say macabre) sense of what he wanted to happened to his body immediately after his death, which took place at his London home on June 6, 1832. He had asked that, in the presence of his friends, his corpse was to be carefully dissected and turned into what was known at the time as an "auto-icon." An auto-icon is essentially a mummified body, such as a taxidermist might create. This is an extract from Bentham's will, now kept in the British National Archives:

My body I give to my dear friend Doctor Southwood Smith to be disposed of in a manner hereinafter mentioned, and I direct...he will take my body under his charge and take the requisite and appropriate measures for the disposal and preservation of the several parts of my bodily frame in the manner expressed in the paper annexed to this my will and at the top of which I have written Auto Icon. The skeleton he will cause to be put together in such a manner as that the whole figure may be seated in a chair usually occupied by me when living, in the attitude in which I am sitting when engaged in thought in the course of time employed in writing. I direct that the body thus prepared shall be transferred to my executor. He will cause the skeleton to be clad in one of the suits of black occasionally worn by me. The body so clothed, together with the chair and the staff in the my later years bourne by me, he will take charge of and for containing the whole apparatus he will cause to be prepared an appropriate box or case and will cause to be engraved in conspicuous characters on a plate to be affixed thereon and also on the labels on the glass cases in which the preparations of the soft parts of my body shall be contained...my name at length with the letters ob: followed by the day of my decease. If it should so happen that my personal friends and other disciples should be disposed to meet together on some day or days of the year for the purpose of commemorating the founder of the greatest happiness system of morals and legislation my executor will from time to time cause to be conveyed to the room in which they meet the said box or case with the contents therein to be stationed in such part of the room as to the assembled company shall seem meet.

Queens Square Place, Westminster, Wednesday 30th May, 1832.

Two days after his death, Bentham's body was indeed cut up in the manner that he had requested. The preserved skeleton was dressed in one of Bentham's best suits, stuffed with hay in order to fill out its appearance somewhat, then given gloves and posed in a seated position, with "Dapple" resting between his knees.

Unfortunately something went badly wrong with Jeremy Bentham's head during the process of preservation. The finished product—complete with glass eyes stuck into the sockets, eyes that Bentham carried around with him in his pockets during the last few years of his life—would not look out of place in a horror movie. The head is so grotesquely zombie-like that it regularly unnerved visitors to the college, and so the decision was made to replace it with a wax substitute that looks far more lifelike and natural.

College students throughout the world are notorious for their love of playing practical jokes and pranks, and this tendency came to a head (if you will pardon the pun) in 1975 when students from a rival college kidnapped Jeremy Bentham's desiccated head and held it for ransom. The ransom was duly paid to the kidnappers' selected charity, and the head was returned safely to its home at University College. But further kidnap attempts ensued, including one memorable incident in which the head was used for football practice! It is now kept safely under lock and key by the college authorities, officially classified as "human remains" that can only be viewed by visitors under rare and exceptional circumstances.

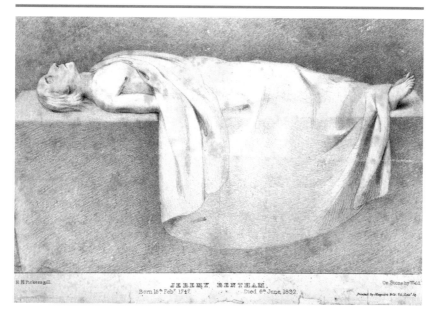

JEREMY BENTHAM.
Born 15ᵗʰ Feb 1747.   Died 6ᵗʰ June 1832.

The newly dead body of Jeremy Bentham, prior to its being dismembered at his request. He is University College Hospital's most famous ghost. Photo courtesy of Wellcome Library, London.

Now permanently displayed in the South Cloisters section of the main college building where it greets visitors, Jeremy Bentham's auto-icon has become such a popular object of curiosity that University College London has created a way for the public to view it online: The "Virtual Auto-icon" allows you to rotate around the mummy in a full circle and view it from a multitude of angles. If you're curious and would like to take a look for yourself, I highly recommend taking the virtual tour.[1]

A number of tall tales have sprung up around the auto-icon through the years, the most popular being that it sometimes attends meetings of the College Council, where (in a typically British display of dry humor), he is said to be "present but not voting," or he is used to cast a tie-breaking vote (Bentham is said to always vote in favor of the motion being presented). Although this makes for a wonderfully colorful tale, in reality the administration of University College London denies that this ever actually happens.

The bizarre and fascinating afterlife of Jeremy Bentham isn't restricted to just his physical remains, however. The great man's ghost has been seen and heard in the corridors of both University College and the hospital that bears its name. In his classic tome *Haunted London,* the great ghost hunter Peter Underwood reports that Bentham's last walking stick, Dapple, has been heard tapping throughout the corridors on winter evenings, along with his heavy footfall on the tiles. His ghost also gets the blame for moving objects around without apparent rhyme or reason in one of the classrooms.

Underwood goes on to recount the tale of mathematics master Neil King, who once heard the sounds of Dapple tapping its way toward his classroom one night. Curiously, Mr. King poked his head out into the corridor and came face to face with the apparition of Jeremy Bentham, working his way toward the mathematics classroom. The ghost seemed to be completely unaware of the flesh-and-blood teacher's presence, but at the last moment: "The form seemed to suddenly dart forward and almost throw itself 'bodily' at the teacher; but there was no sensation of impact and then King realized that all sight and sound of Jeremy Bentham had disappeared.[2]

The staff at University College Hospital has also encountered the apparition of Jeremy Bentham, once again happening upon his distinctive form as it roams the corridors and hallways, sometimes following the startled employees as they go about their daily business. The ghost sometimes waves Dapple at them, though whether trying to simply attract their attention, or to convey some kind of message to them, it is impossible to say.

It would seem that Jeremy is enjoying an afterlife that is every bit as eccentric and active as his physical life once was!

CHAPTER 11

The Yorktown Memorial Hospital
Yorktown, Texas, USA

ocated some 75 miles southeast of San Antonio, Texas, is the picturesque city of Yorktown. Small and friendly, Yorktown is home to a little more than 2,000 people. It was founded in 1848 and named after a famous Indian fighter named Captain John York (although the city's most famous son is undoubtedly Harlon Block, a United States Marine who was pictured raising the Stars and Stripes on Iwo Jima in one of the 20th century's most iconic photographs).

Constructed in 1950 and opened in 1951, the Yorktown Memorial Hospital was a shining example of what can be achieved when the public collectively comes together in the service of the greater good. Prior to 1951, Yorktown residents (and those from the surrounding towns) who were either sick or injured were forced to drive at least 30 miles in order to seek treatment—sometimes dying along the way if their condition was serious enough. Seeing a clear need for a hospital facility somewhat closer to home, Yorktown area residents and the Felician Sisters of the Roman Catholic Church conducted a "politely aggressive" fundraising campaign in order to raise the money needed to fund a facility in their own city.

"Many hands must toil," declared a lavish fundraising pamphlet distributed to local citizens and businesses in 1949. "...and all of our efforts be combined before this beautiful building becomes, in actuality, the Yorktown Memorial Hospital," it continued. "It cannot be completed through the work and determination of a few—even their great sacrifice would be a puny offering toward the great job to be done. Yorktown is determined that the project—a memorial to the war dead of two great conflicts—shall be speedily finished.

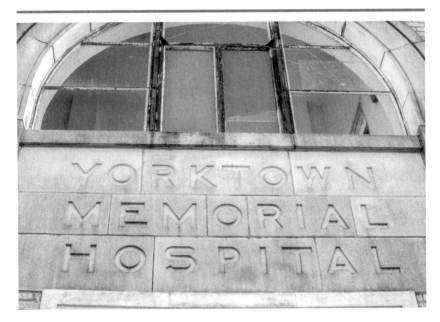

Yorktown Memorial's signage. Photo courtesy of Amber Moose.

The task belongs to each of us, and the burden of responsibility and accomplishment likewise is ours."

Land was donated for the hospital, and sizable cash donations were made by the Felician Sisters, as well as the charitable arm of the Ford Motor Company. Numerous private citizens and small business owners contributed money to what became a landmark community project. At full capacity, the hospital could handle 21 admitted patients, and also had a number of specialist capabilities, such as obstetric and gynecological services devoted to delivering babies. There was also a state-of-the-art X-ray suite.

Supplanted by a larger competing hospital, Yorktown Memorial finally closed its doors for good in 1987, having served the public for the better part of 36 years. Estimates vary on just how many patients died within its walls during that time, but the best approximation lies somewhere around 2,000, according to a general practice physician who worked there.

The hospital building did not stand idle for long, as it was converted for use as a drug and alcohol rehabilitation clinic. The state was soon forced to close down, due to one too many reports of its uncontrollable patients causing problems, according to *The Russell Rush Haunted Tour*.[1] A triple stabbing/double murder supposedly took place in the basement of the rehab facility. A female drug treatment counselor was romantically involved with two men, but reports vary as to whether both were patients, or one was a patient while the other was a colleague. Whichever is the case, one of the males found the other two members of this particular love triangle together in the basement, and in a fit of rage stabbed them both, killing the woman and wounding the man.

Fighting for his life, the man who had been stabbed grappled with his would-be killer, somehow managing to wrest the knife out of his grasp, and then stabbed him to death in return. Blood stains that are said to be a remnant from that violent and sordid knife frenzy can still be seen today, splattered across the brick walls of the basement—though things are not quite as they seem when it comes to this blood, as we shall soon see.

In the spring of 2011, investigators from the Golden Crescent Paranormal research group locked themselves inside the Yorktown Memorial Hospital in an attempt to uncover some of its secrets. So impressed were they with the results that Golden Crescent would return to Yorktown five more times in total.

Group founder and investigator Rob Calzada remains skeptical of some of the ghost lore surrounding the hospital, in particular the tales regarding the murders down in the basement. In a phone interview conducted during the writing of this book, Rob told me that "our historical research could not validate that the murders in the basement ever actually took place." His team had examined as much documentation as possible in trying to uncover evidence of the murder, all to no avail. "The police department said they knew nothing about it. I think that it's just an urban legend."

"But what about the bloodstains sprayed all over the basement wall?" I challenged him.

"We actually went in there, got a cotton swab, took a sample of it down to the police station to get it tested," Rob explained. "They found out that it was *animal blood*."

It wasn't to be long before Rob was hearing disembodied voices with his own ears, as the team started to investigate the haunted basement. Calzada was all by himself at one end, with all of his colleagues clustered at the opposite end of the hallway. As he was picking up a camcorder that he had briefly set down on the floor, Rob felt what he describes as a "cobwebby sensation" on his skin. All alone and shrouded in absolute darkness, the seasoned investigator was startled to hear a voice located directly behind his ear intone just one chilling word:

"Rob."

As his fellow investigators quickly converged upon his position, the same voice spoke something in a foreign language, the specifics of which Calzada could not identify. "It sounded like German, or Italian, something like that," he told me. "But it definitely sounded like it wanted me to *get out*."

A photograph taken of Rob at the time showed an unusual light anomaly positioned directly next to him. He finds the combination of the cobweb sensation, the light anomaly, and the voice to be very persuasive evidence of paranormal forces at work in the basement of Yorktown Memorial. Hospital legend has it that the basement is also haunted by a kindly ghost nicknamed "Papa" (his real name has never been uncovered). The story goes that Papa was once a maintenance worker at Yorktown Memorial, and though I could uncover no reports of his ghost actually making an appearance, the disembodied whistling that is frequently heard down in the basement is usually attributed to him.

Digital voice recorders left running in the empty basement overnight by the *Ghost Adventures* team during their lockdown at Yorktown Memorial recorded what sounds eerily like the plaintive wail of a woman in distress, as though she was crying out in either pain or despair.

Lead investigator Jason Arnold of Contact Paranormal Research tells a different version of the basement murder story. According to Jason, the female was named Debbie, a nurse who just happened to be escorting two patients down to the rehab area in the basement one day, when one of them suddenly whipped out a knife. Both Debbie and the other patient were supposedly stabbed repeatedly, and the rest of the story is consistent with what we have already heard—Debbie and her attacker died at the scene. This is, of course, just a variation on the tale, but in this case there is no "love triangle" aspect to the story. The truth remains unclear, and probably always will.

I have both personally investigated and collected eyewitness reports concerning hundreds of haunted properties during my two decades of assessing claims of the paranormal. During that time, I have encountered many truly unique and bizarre haunted locations, but never before have I heard of a *guard donkey,* a walking, kicking security system who used to roam the grounds at Yorktown Memorial. "Spirit Yorktown" rose to popularity after sauntering up on Zak Bagans and the *Ghost Adventures* crew during their lockdown at Yorktown Memorial, and became something of a minor Internet celebrity afterward. Spirit had his own Facebook page, in which he listed his job as "security" for the hospital, and perhaps more worryingly, described his relationship status as "It's Complicated."

"Hey everybody! Sorry I've been away for a while. Vandals & pranksters, as well as the occasional ghosts have been keeping me very busy! Thanks for everyone's continued support!" So went a fairly typical Facebook status update. Sadly, Spirit's life story had a sad and tragic ending when he was fatally poisoned by persons unknown. His remains are buried close to Mike's trailer (see page 159). One has to wonder whether Spirit's spirit has remained behind to guard the Yorktown Memorial Hospital campus for as long as it remains standing.

During a September 2011 interview with journalist Roberto Ontiveros, the hospital's owner, real estate broker and attorney Phil Ross, says that he originally bought the place as a potential warehouse, but it did not take long for the reports of paranormal occurrences to start piling up. A team of psychic investigators whom Ross asked to investigate the hospital were soon assaulted with the sensation of being choked by invisible hands, and exposed to "all sorts of violent imagery and disturbing things."[2]

In regard to some of the Earth-bound spirits that she encountered during a visit to Yorktown Memorial, Ontiveros' article quotes local paranormal investigator Jo Marks-Rivera. "One of them kept telling us to 'Get the f--- out of here,' but when we talked to him we understood that he was trying to warn us. He had been butchered by a 'Dr. --------' during a thyroid operation and was trying to help us out, keep us safe."

I have removed the doctor's name from this quote simply because there are two sides to every story, and it would be unfair to tarnish a physician's reputation without more in the way of tangible evidence. But this doctor is also referred to by *The Russell Rush Haunted Tour* as one of the resident ghosts who haunts Yorktown Memorial, having died shortly after his retirement. His shadowy apparition was seen walking past the doorway to the physician's lounge on at least one occasion by one of his astonished flesh-and-blood colleagues.

"I couldn't see a face, I couldn't see details," said Dr. Gordon Barth, a general practice physician who had the distinction of not only practicing medicine at Yorktown Memorial, but was also born there. When interviewed by Zak Bagans shortly before their 2011 lockdown at the hospital, Dr. Barth talked about his encounter with the ghostly doctor. "But I saw a silhouette that made me think it was [him]. When I got up and looked again, he was gone." Every time Dr. Barth took a nap afterward, he would check the corridor first to make sure that nobody was standing there.

Eyewitness testimony from doctors and other healthcare providers is usually given great weight by paranormal investigators. Such medical professionals tend to be well-educated and have strong critical thinking skills, have a keen eye for detail, and are also capable of keeping their head in a crisis. Dr. Barth is not a believer in ghosts or the paranormal, but admits that he experienced a number of strange events at Yorktown Memorial that he cannot explain.

Rob Calzada of Golden Crescent Paranormal believes that he and his teammates (accompanied by Mike the caretaker) may have run into the spirit of this particular doctor during their pre-investigation walk-through of the building. Strangely, this encounter with an almost full body male apparition happened during broad daylight.

"We were at the other end of the hallway, looking down toward the Doctors' Lounge. We had a complete view of the corridor. Mike and I were in front, with the other two members behind us. We looked down the hall, Mike and I, and we actually saw a doctor in a white coat walk from the Emergency Room into the Doctors' Lounge! Whatever this was had on a white coat, *no legs whatsoever,* and the head was blurred.

"Mike and I turned to each other. We had no equipment, because the investigation hadn't started yet. And we asked each other, 'Did you see that?' We immediately compared notes and found out that we had both seen the same thing. The sun was out, and we both saw him as clear as day. You could *clearly* make out that it was a doctor in a lab coat. And this was where the ghost of the doctor has always been seen."

Impressed, I asked Rob whether the apparition was solid like a flesh and blood person, or whether it had some degree of transparency. "You could see through the white coat," he answered levelly. "The head was fuzzy. That was probably the single most impressive experience we had there at Yorktown Memorial."

Paranormal investigator Susan Wallner, founder of the Final Dimension Paranormal team, has been to Yorktown Memorial so many times that she has lost count. "It is a great place for me to train new investigators," says Susan, "because it will either make them, or break them quick!"

On the first of many visits to Yorktown Memorial, Susan was conducting some flashlight experiments in the office of this particular doctor, which is located on the first floor near to the entrance lobby. For those who might be unfamiliar with this particular technique, flashlight experimentation involves requesting any spirits present to manipulate a flashlight in order to answer questions, turning it off and on in some agreed-to pattern, such as one flash for yes, two flashes for no. It is a simple technique that sometimes yields fascinating results. Susan and her fellow investigators used multiple flashlights—necessary in order to rule out mechanical issues as the cause of the lights flashing—and were able to get yes/no answers to their questions.

But the apparitions seen in the hospital are not restricted to just those of the doctors. For example, the ghost of a former lab technician named Jacob has been sighted in the same area as that of the white-coated doctor, walking past the physicians' lounge and passing through the lab area in which he once ran tests during his lifetime.

It is only fitting, given the facility's close tie with the Felician Sisters of the Roman Catholic Church, that a ghostly nun wearing a dark habit has also been seen drifting through the now-deserted corridors.

Yorktown Memorial Hospital's tour coordinator and overall groundskeeper is named Mike. Living in a trailer on the grounds and spending a great deal of time there, one would expect Mike to be the authority on whether the old hospital is haunted or not. He told interviewer Zak Bagans unequivocally that the hospital had ghosts—the good kind, and the bad kind. Mike related paranormal attacks taking place there, with people being slapped, punched, and kicked. Scratching and choking by unseen assailants is another common and frightening occurrence, happening most often upstairs in what is known as the "nuns' lounge" or "nuns' corridor." Investigators and visitors have pointed out through the years that quite a few of the attacks seem to center upon people with tattoos and other such body markings.[3] Could it be that somehow, some remnant of the nuns who used to work in that area still disapproves of the manner in which those uninvited visitors have chosen to adorn their body?

Investigator Susan Wallner doesn't buy into the tattoo theory. "I have seen and been with plenty of people that have tattoos and plenty that don't," Susan told me, "and the same things happen either way, so I don't think that it's a deciding factor. It seems to me that the more respect we show while in that area, the more evidence and communication we tend to get."

In a clear-cut example of "be careful what you wish for," one paranormal investigator was asking one of the child spirits who haunts the hospital—a young girl by the name of Stacey—to make her presence known to him, or to give him a sign of her existence. According to ghost hunter Jason Arnold, Stacey was a patient in the hospital who unfortunately passed away there from unknown causes. Following a high-pitched, child-like giggle, a rock was hurled directly at the surprised investigator, who quite understandably fled the building at great speed.

Jason's story is further corroborated by Susan Wallner, who believes that she has actually seen Stacey make an appearance once, crossing the basement hallway. Things turned from light-hearted to dark very quickly one night, when Susan and her team were trying to communicate with the spirit of this young girl. "It seemed as though I was communicating with Stacy through the Ghost Box," Susan says, "and it went great for a few minutes. Then another voice came through that was most certainly NOT a little girl, and threatened us. We could hear a girl's cry at the same time. I demanded that it leave Stacey alone and let her talk with us, but it did not cooperate. I then called upon Doug, again, and he seemed to have been able to get her to safety. It was a very bizarre event, and one that I will not soon forget." (We will learn about the ghost named Doug next.)

According to Rob Calzada, Stacey spends most of her time up on the first floor, but has also been known to venture down into the basement. He told me of one incident in which he and another investigator were at the bottom of the basement stairs, getting ready to climb up. They were talking to one another in hushed tones with a digital voice recorder running in the background. When the audio files were reviewed after the investigation, a child-like voice could be heard mimicking their words and mannerisms, repeating them back in the way that young children often seem to find so amusing.

One of the most frequently reported ghosts is that of a man named Doug Richards, a heavy equipment mechanic who died in 1973. He sometimes appears on demand, as a pair of shocked investigators found out when they called out to him by name in one of the corridors, only to see a large shadow figure (" a very, very large man") crossing at the end of the hallway.

Mike has conducted quite a few electronic voice phenomena experiments with Doug, and claims that this particular spirit has even gotten right up into Mike's face and waved his fingers just inches away from his eyes.

"He's as curious about us as we are about him," Mike says. "I asked him: 'Where do you hang out mostly?' and he answers, 'In the basement.'"[4] Mike also captured a Class A EVP (Class A means that is of the highest quality and clarity), which followed a request for Doug to state his own name. The voice on the recording is quite clearly heard to reply, "Doug!"

Susan Waller has her own thoughts about Doug:

Doug is without a doubt, my absolute favorite resident. Nobody seems to know where he came from at all but have only found him in the basement. I have been told that he only calls two people by name, and I am lucky enough to be one of them. We have caught multiple EVPs where I can address him and ask him if he knows who I am or if he can say my name and he does more often than not. Also, when I ask that he say his name for us so that I know who we are talking to, he will reply with a recorded EVP or on the Ghost Box. I tend to consider him my protector when I'm there as well because of something that happened one night when we were there.

I was down the hall in the basement, and a group of four investigators was at the other end of the hall in the laundry room, using the Ghost Box. One of the investigators called to me to get down there because my name kept coming over the box. When I did, I started asking questions to see who it was. Well, when nothing came through, I got a bit aggravated with it and said something to the extent of 'you get me down here and then you stop talking? Are you scared now that I'm here?' The room temperature felt as though it dropped about 15 degrees and went even darker than it had already been. Well, it quickly spit out three words—"f*** you, b****." Needless to say I was immediately shaken. When suddenly, a different voice came through and said *"Susan, leave!"* which I believed to be Doug.

We got out of there fast! That's the first of only two instances that I've ever needed to step outside of the hospital to gather my bearings. Three of the four investigators that were there when it happened actually left, refusing to go back in the building, even to retrieve their personal belongings. I have also seen Doug. I had a group of people with me in the basement that had never been to the hospital before. I was telling them all about Doug and the things that he had done for us in the past. I asked him to please come out and meet my friends that had come to meet him. After a few requests and a few minutes, across the end of the hall, walked a full-bodied dark human shape that looked to be very broad and no shorter than 6'5". It was amazing! I thanked him of course and from the same area where we saw the shadow cross the hall, a sound came as if to respond.

When I interviewed Susan for this book, she seemed almost nostalgic and protective of this harmless hospital ghost, telling me that she likes to return as often as possible to visit with him. It came across in much the same way as one might speak of a distant but much-missed relative, for whom she obviously has great affection.

Susan is the proud owner of a class A EVP recording, that rarest type of EVPs—one that is so clearly and distinctly a human voice that skeptics cannot simply write it off as background noise or meaningless static. When asking Doug specifically to speak his name into the digital voice recorder, she received the clear and distinct response: "Doug." Susan regards this as the most impressive piece of evidence that she has received at Yorktown Memorial, because "the group that I had in the room with me was just totally floored by how fluid it was, how comfortable the environment was and then to get that someone else was there with us that we couldn't see, to them, was the Holy Grail, if you will."

Rob Calzada and his colleagues may also have encountered the ghost of big Doug Richards when they were down in the hospital basement. As they were gathering up some infrared camera equipment that they had previously left down there, a female investigator looked down toward the end of the gloomy hallway, where she saw what she described as a "darker than dark mass" standing there, simply looking at her. The mass was an estimated 6 feet, 6 inches in height, and in the shape of a human body. The incredulous ghost hunter quickly gathered up the equipment and ran back upstairs.

During the course of their lockdown, Zak Bagans and the *Ghost Adventures* investigators captured on camera what appears to be a shadowy form lurking in one of the corridors. The figure *was* also seen with Bagans's own eyes (most ghostly figures that later appear on camera are not seen at the time the photograph was taken) and sudden spikes in electromagnetic energy followed almost immediately.

Jason Arnold and his colleagues Angela, Cathy, and Thomas, from the Houston-based Contact Paranormal Research team, investigated the old Yorktown Memorial Hospital over several nights in 2014, describing it as "one of the most active places we have ever been to."

The crew from Contact Paranormal varied their research methods by mixing up the number of investigators in the building at various times, on some occasions going so far as to have only one person in the building alone.

I asked the investigators about the first night that they spent shut inside the ramshackle old hospital. "First night as we were setting up at base camp," says Jason, "one of our investigators, Thomas, saw a grey shadow pass in front of the chapel. Later we found out they call him 'The Grey Man.'"

For the first hour of their investigation, Jason was keeping vigil outside the priest's quarters down in the basement, and was fortunate enough to hear the sound of three disembodied footsteps in the area. He also saw a blue light coalesce in the same place, just outside the entrance doorway. Clustered upstairs in the chapel and the area set aside for delivering babies, the rest of the team experienced nothing even remotely as memorable. But they had no way of knowing that ultimately, Yorktown Memorial was not going to disappoint them....

"On the first night, it just felt like an abandoned hospital, dusty and dark with a slight smell of mildew," Jason explained. "But when we showed up on the second night, it felt like it was *alive*. It was like we woke it up the night before. There was a heavy feeling in the air that gave you a sense of uneasiness. A few investigators felt as if we were being watched."

They noticed that the atmosphere inside the ramshackle old building felt different on the second night of their 48 hour visit when they had fewer investigators inside. It was quiet at first, but slowly became more active as the evening wore on.

Something invisible (nothing was caught on the video monitors) was heard to slide across the hallway, with only one investigator being present in the building—and unbeknownst to this brave individual, the sound of footsteps was recorded coming up the staircase at that very same time. The investigator did not hear those footsteps when they were happening, finding out only upon playback and review of the digital sound recordings. As evidence goes, this particular EVP is made more impressive by the fact that it was caught not only on digital voice recorders, but also on the feed from the camera that was covering that particular corridor—a corridor in which absolutely nothing was seen to be moving that could account for those sounds.[5]

When the crew from Contact Paranormal Research discussed these footsteps with Mike the caretaker the following day, he told them in a very matter-of-fact way that the footsteps were a daily occurrence at Yorktown Memorial. Mike remains convinced that this is the ghost of the caretaker who looked after the hospital before he did, described as "a heavy-footed man" who walked along that same pathway every day until his death.

Nor was this to be the only auditory phenomena that they captured. The squeaking noise of a gurney or medicine cart of some kind was also recorded. The sounds seemed to advance up to the doorway of what was once the pharmacy, before going back again in the direction from which it had come. As we shall see in a later chapter, there are shades of Singapore's old Changi Hospital here, in which investigators have also recorded the sound of gurneys and wheelchairs. Piano keys were both heard and recorded at Yorktown, along with a broad array of other noises in what should have been a peaceful and quiet old building. Could somebody of flesh and blood have snuck into the hospital unseen, evading not only the investigators, but also Mike the Caretaker and Spirit the donkey, in order to play a trick on them all by making a bit of noise? Impossible, declares Jason, because observers were posted at each end of the corridor at the time of the recording, and all was still and quiet.

The sound of the cart wheels squeaking was something completely new to Mike, and he was very impressed with the recording when it was played back to him. Determined to rule out any natural causes, the four investigators split up and scrutinized each and every wheeled cart, chair, table, and trash bin in the entire building, in an attempt to replicate the noise. Having been unsuccessful inside the hospital building itself, they went one step further and expanded their search to the outside grounds—all to no avail. Nothing sounded like the noise that they had recorded. After the investigation, Jason and his team even went so far as to contact the Felician Sisters directly. They were intrigued to learn from the Sisters that the old medical carts that they had use in the hospital were notoriously prone to getting squeaky with age and wear and tear.

Jason and his team believe that the two most active spirits haunting Yorktown Memorial are both female—one being the ghost of young Stacey whom we encountered earlier, and the other being Debbie, the woman who was supposedly stabbed to death down in the basement. Both of these spirits have responded to several questions asked by the investigators during EVP sessions. Whereas their answers are a little longer than the average EVP, and sometimes form complete sentences ("It's time to leave us alone") the disembodied male-sounding voices recorded by Contact Paranormal at Yorktown appear to be more clipped and terse, such as the one that seemed to growl "You should be afraid...."

Who is the owner of this angry male voice that has imprinted itself on the digital recordings made by the Contact Paranormal investigators? Jason's theory is an intriguing one. He believes the voice belongs to the murderer that stabbed Debbie to death down in the basement, before finally meeting his own demise in a similarly violent fashion.

"All the research we have done on Yorktown always leads us back to the man who killed Debbie," Jason says. "We have yet to find a name of the attacker. But he was the only one who died at the hospital in such violent way. We allowed Mike to listen to a lot of the EVPs and he agreed that this is the man who killed Debbie. This information comes from Mike's own experiences and that of other teams who have investigated the hospital."

The Holy Grail for every ghost hunter is, of course, to see a full-body apparition, and some of the Contact Paranormal investigators were to be rewarded for their patience by sighting the ghost of the so-called "Grey Man." Just who *is* this mysterious spirit? Neither the team from Contact Paranormal, nor Mike the caretaker, are aware of the Grey Man's identity, but he has been seen frequently within the walls of the old hospital, wandering aimlessly through the deserted rooms and hallways. By far the most common location in which he is seen is the doorway to the chapel, where witnesses report that he often lingers before abruptly darting away and disappearing into the shadows. Jason explains:

> Thomas first sighted him as we were standing outside of base camp directly down the hallway from the chapel. He caught a glimpse of movement out of the corner of his eye and instantly turned to see it walk out of sight to the right side of the doorway. He proceeded to check the area and found no one. All the investigators were at base camp at that time. The area in front of the chapel is very dark and when he is in the area his shadow has a grayish hue to it. It lightens the area and you can clearly see the outline before he vanishes. The area started to lighten and then there was the outline of what appeared to be a man standing in the doorway, and as fast as it appeared, it was gone. He checked the area to find no one. Jose's sighting happened exactly as Thomas's did. The only difference was it was on the second trip to the Hospital. We found out from Mike that this happens to him and other investigators all the time.

Incredibly, this encounter with the Grey Man was not the only apparition that the team from Contract Paranormal Research would encounter during their time at Yorktown Memorial. The patient named T.J., whose dead body was abandoned outside the hospital doors, was also intent upon making his presence felt. Lead investigator Jason once again takes up the story:

> We just finished up the investigation and Jason and Thomas were waiting for Mike to come lock up behind us. Jason was standing in the hallway facing the afterhours ER entrance and Thomas was facing the front entrance of the Hospital. Mike appears at the afterhours ER entrance and walks down the hallway toward them. After reaching them, he asked how the night had been. Right at that moment Jason said 'Did you hear that?' and both Thomas and Mike replied that they had not.

Some of the original gurneys can still be found inside the corridors of Yorktown Memorial. Photo courtesy of Amber Moose.

At that same time, Jason and Mike saw the apparition standing in the hallway right next to the after-hours Emergency Room entrance. He was fully clothed and was staring straight at us. He was there for only a second and gone right before our eyes. He appeared to be wearing blue jeans and a darkish long sleeve shirt. Thomas did not see the apparition, as he was facing toward the front entrance. Mike said that this is a figure he sees on a regular basis and believes it to be T.J., a man who died after being dropped off at the entrance.

When the hospital was still operational, the Emergency Room doors would be closed and locked at 10 o'clock each night, and any prospective patient would have to ring a bell mounted on the wall in order to get help. Whether the bell was never rung on a particular Friday night, or perhaps the nun assigned to night duty never heard it ring, is something of which we can never be sure. But what *is* known is that when the emergency room doors were opened up for business one Saturday morning, T.J.'s body was found sprawled on the ground outside them. He had died of a heroin overdose. His ghost is most commonly seen in and around the area of the Emergency Room.

Returning to the tendency of visitors who have tattoos to experience paranormal activity when passing through the nuns' quarters (sometimes very disturbing activity at that), Rob Calzada would later have his own paranormal encounter in that upstairs section of the hospital, feeling faint and weak with no apparent cause.

At almost exactly the same time that Calzada started to feel dizzy and light-headed in the nuns' corridors upstairs, his fellow investigators were getting anomalously high EMF readings in that same part of the building. Although he wasn't getting choked or physically hit as others have, electromagnetic energy levels kept spiking when he made reference to the tattoos on both his arms. Back in the days when the hospital was still operational, the nuns' corridors and surrounding areas were strictly off-limits to all males. A popular theory among investigators who have been attacked at Yorktown Memorial is that putting men—especially *tattooed* men—into that particular region of the hospital is an almost sure-fire way to provoke some type of disapproving response from the ghostly inhabitants.

"Everyone with tattoos on them *did* have things happen to them, up there in the nuns' quarters," Rob confirmed for me during our interview. "And the ones that had no tattoos...well, nothing occurred with them."

The array of activity that was experienced by the tattooed investigators is intriguing. Their legs would suddenly get weak, beginning to shake and tremble. They broke out into tears for no apparent reason, weeping sorrowfully. More alarmingly, when those investigators were photographed up in the nuns' quarters, their faces bore expressions of uncharacteristic anger and rage. It sounds as though those investigators without tattoos got off rather lightly by comparison.

Perhaps the most chilling EVP captured during the investigation happened outside the Labor and Delivery bay. Rob and his daughter were running a digital voice recorder when she pointed to a nearby wheelchair and asked whether it would be considered bad luck for one of them to sit down in it. No sooner had Rob expressed his opinion that it would not be unlucky than a voice providing an answer was clearly imprinted on the audio file: "There's somebody sitting in that chair."

Equipment liked to behave oddly during the Golden Crescent investigation. Flashlights developed a disconcerting tendency to switch themselves on and off again, particularly in the area of the kitchens.

Although Zak Bagans and the *Ghost Adventures* crew seem to have captured one of the best instances of an apparition at Yorktown Memorial in the form of the figure seen lurking in one of the corridors, some intriguing light anomalies have been captured on camera by other investigative teams. For example, a group from *The Russell*

Rush Haunted Tour spent several nights there, taking hundreds of photographs across all of the floors.

The vast majority of so-called "light anomalies" can easily be explained away by the tendency of light from a camera's flash bouncing back from dust particles at a very narrow angle. But a select few may defy such simple explanation. The *Russell Rush* team appears to have captured some interesting solid, glowing balls of light in the corridors and basement area of the old hospital— varying in both color and density. As with any apparently anomalous photograph, it's impossible to rule out natural causes such as environmental sources of ambient light, but even so, their Yorktown Memorial photos are fascinating. I encourage you to make up your own mind by checking out the gallery posted over at *www.therussell rushhauntedtour.com.*

Russell Rush and his team also recorded the sound of a scream originating in the Labor and Delivery room, which was the scene of hundreds, if not thousands of newborn babies delivered over the course of the hospital's lifetime. However, all of the truly compelling stories surrounding Yorktown Memorial do not center upon those who entered this world from within its walls, but rather from those who have died there. It would seem that some of them are not yet ready to move on to whatever it is that comes next.

There are so many areas within Yorktown Memorial that have experienced paranormal activity that it is difficult to pin down the most haunted spot. One place that has a strong claim to that title is the boiler room. Susan Wallner is convinced that a dark, evil being resides in there.

I feel as though I am warned each and every time that I enter that room—warned that I shouldn't be there, and that if I choose to be, I will know that I am not at all welcome. I have left that room on more than one investigation due to feelings of nausea, dizziness, legitimate fear. It doesn't seem to affect most other people that way, other than the fact that they are very scared in there and ready to get out. I'm not sure if I feel all of that because I try a bit harder to get through to whatever is there and it just wants to hide. But I can tell you this ...if you provoke or piss it off, it has no problem whatsoever coming out of that room after you....

One example of this is the time in which Susan and her fellow investigators were sitting in the area of the basement that is nicknamed "the four-way," a convergence of four corridors located just outside the boiler room. The small group had just left the boiler room a few minutes before and she confessed to feeling uneasy, without knowing precisely why. She was about to find out.

It took several minutes to escalate but when it did, oh man! We watched things get darker. The air around us was heavier, and several of us were having a hard time breathing. I told the other team members that "it" was in there with us. I knew it was, and it was *angry*. Finally, when we knew that none of us could really handle any more and were at our absolute end of sanity because the environment was changing so drastically and affecting each and every one of us in that area, something, "it" from the boiler room, grabbed ahold of my thigh with such force that I thought I had been nailed to the tile floor. Although the grip lasted probably no more than seconds, it seemed as though it was a lifetime.

I was in total shock and literally yelled out which, again, I had never done before. My fellow investigators knew when I yelled that there was something terribly wrong. I cleared everyone out of the area and we did not return to the basement for the rest of the night. And that was the second of only two times that I was literally forced from the building to get myself together. I do not pursue the boiler room for I feel that the evil that is there will do whatever it needs to in order to maintain "Its" space. I do not feel that it is necessary to put myself, or other investigators, in that situation, and so I choose not to. Now don't get me wrong, I do still go to the basement every time that I'm there as it is my favorite area. I just don't cross the threshold of the boiler room anymore. I see it as I was warned and I'd better not forget that.

Investigator Hazel Bishop and her colleagues from the West Houston Paranormal Society experienced a little more than they bargained for during their investigation at Yorktown Memorial. One member of her team donned a nun's habit in the chapel. If this was intended to provoke a response, it succeeded: the investigator received a slap from something unseen for their trouble! A female investigator who entered the Mother Superior's former room claimed to be choked, again by invisible hands. "It is said that you must knock before entering," says Hazel, "and we did not." It is also worth pointing out that this lady had her tattoos visible when she was attacked.

Equally disturbing is the investigator who received a series of scratches when the team was looking around in the basement. In the same location, a ball that was being used as a control object began to move all by itself. A request to drop the temperature by a few degrees was granted by whatever it is that haunts the old operating room. Yorktown Memorial was firing on all cylinders for the folks from W.H.P.S.

"Several different investigators suffered a sense of spiritual oppression at different points of our investigation," Hazel concludes. "We caught what sounds like an announcement coming over the disconnected P.A. system in the building, which was quite chilling. We also recorded a moaning coming from Labor and Delivery. This is a fantastic place for an investigation. The hospital has given us some amazing personal experiences, and we have never left there empty-handed."

As we have seen, Yorktown Memorial has a strong claim to being one of the world's most haunted hospitals. I will leave the last word to long-term Yorktown Memorial researcher Susan Wallner. "It's actually an amazing place," she says. "Not only from a paranormal standpoint, but from a historical, architectural, and religious view as well. Everything that the hospital accomplished and represented in that small town is really an amazing feat to be admired."

For more information, check out *www.richardestep.net/books /the-worlds-most-haunted-hospitals/* where you can find additional bonus content and interviews on this topic.

CHAPTER 12

The Danvers State Insane Asylum
Danvers, Massachusetts, USA

If you happened to be standing at the foot of Hathorne Hill in Danvers, Massachusetts, on a particularly dark and stormy night, you could quite easily be forgiven for thinking that you had stepped onto the set of a Gothic horror film of some sort. The four-story building that loomed menacingly above you on the hilltop would have made the perfect lair for a mad scientist in the mold of Victor Frankenstein, cackling maniacally in the candle-lit window of one of its turreted towers.

Originally known by the fonder name of "the castle on the hill," Danvers went on to acquire a darker reputation as the years passed by. "The Haunted Castle" and "The Witches Castle" are just two of the nicknames given by the local residents to the huge edifice that holds such a prominent position watching over the entire area for miles around.

Why "The Witches Castle"? Peering backward through the mists of time, the keen student of history will soon discover that the town of Danvers once went by a different name: Salem Village. This is the same Salem Village that was to become the scene of one of the most brutal and terrifying episodes of American history, the 1692 Salem Witch Trials.

During the 21st century, some Christians believed that Satan existed as a kind of abstract force for evil, working behind the scenes to achieve his nefarious ends. But to the pastoral folk of Salem Village at the close of the 17th century, the devil and his army of demons were believed to be very real; physical creatures who were thought to stalk the darkness, preying upon the unwary and always ready to attack the righteous if the mood should take them. Three hundred years ago, fire, brimstone, and damnation were at the forefront of the pious American citizen's mind. There were no horror movies to serve as entertainment—the horror was thought to be very real, and lurking in their midst.

When we consider this atmosphere of constant fear, which served as a backdrop to everyday life, it should come as no surprise at all that the first rumors of witchcraft that were whispered by the townsfolk of Salem Village were spread with all the terrifying rapidity—and hunger for violence—of a raging wildfire. The match was struck by the increasingly bizarre behavior of two young girls, who took to throwing fits, hurling objects, screeching violently, and twisting their bodies into the most peculiar shapes. Though the village doctor examined the girls and confessed his puzzlement, it was not long before the symptoms began to take hold in some of the other women in Salem Village. (Historians have since put forth several possible explanations for the girls' strange behavior including: hallucinogenic chemicals.)

Seeking convenient scapegoats for the outbreak of unnatural maladies, the villagers soon began to point the finger at a trio of unpopular women, declaring them to be witches who were in a league with the Devil and his horde of Satanic minions. As the allegations against the three women became increasingly outrageous—such as conducting sexual liaisons with demonic creatures—a number of townsfolk from Salem Village and the surrounding area rose up to challenge the accusers, only to be branded as witches themselves. These witches were firmly believed to be causing farmers' crops to suffer blight, illnesses and maladies to befall their fellow villagers, and even causing people to die in some cases.

The inquisition had now begun to gather steam, and the arrests continued throughout the long, hot summer of 1692, now including local men as well as women. As juries began to find the defendants guilty, the first executions started to take place. Although still under the rule of the English crown, hysteria was now the true king of Salem Village. The most brutal and vicious forms of torture were employed in order to extract confessions until, half-crazed with the agonies inflicted upon them by their tormentors, the accused would confess to literally *anything* in order to make the pain stop.

Although Hollywood movies have firmly cemented the image of accused witches being burned at the stake into the public consciousness, the truth of the matter is that most were hanged. Of the 140 accused of witchcraft in Salem Village and the surrounding area, 19 would go to the gallows and pay the ultimate price after the hangman's noose was tightened around their necks. One unfortunate soul, Giles Corey, flatly refused to declare his innocence *or* his guilt, failing to enter any plea whatsoever before the court. As the law of the time stated that a defendant who did not enter a plea could not be tried, the workaround used to prevent the presumably guilty defendant from escaping the clutches of justice was a barbaric practice known as *pressing*: Stripped naked, the accused was made to lay down on the floor with a solid wooden plank on top of him. Strong men would load a succession of heavy weights (usually boulders) on top of the wooden surface, until the accumulated weight was unbearably heavy. To make it worse, the poor man was placed on a starvation diet. The pressing went on until the victim either confessed to his crimes, or died.

It is practically impossible to imagine the agony endured by Giles Corey, already in his seventh decade of life, during the two days that he spent being pressed in an attempt to make him confess to practicing witchcraft. When his torturers came back repeatedly to try and extract a confession, the stubborn old man (contemporary accounts tell us that his eyes and tongue were bulging out of his face due to the pressure) simply demanded that they add more weight. Men even stood on top of the plank, adding their own body mass to that of the rocks, crushing his body into the earth. He died without ever making a confession.

Local legend has it that the apparition of Giles Corey is seen walking the graveyard on Howard Street, in the city of Salem (not to be confused with Salem Village, which is now Danvers) whenever a tragedy or disaster is due to befall the city. For example, the apparition of an old man was reported to be drifting through the cemetery at the end of June 1914. Shortly afterward, the Great Fire of Salem tore through the city, laying waste to almost 1,400 buildings.

By the spring of 1693, the hysteria subsided and it was all over. Restitution would ultimately be paid by the State of Massachusetts to those accused who had survived.

The State of Massachusetts did not formally apologize for the Salem Witch Trials until 1957—and even then, not all of the accused were named by the State. Finally, more than 300 years later, in 2001, the Governor of Massachusetts signed a resolution that declared *all*

The unfortunate Giles Corey was brutally "pressed" to death with heavy stones. IMAGE COURTESY OF WIKIMEDIA COMMONS, PUBLIC DOMAIN.

of those accused to be innocent, closing the book on one of the most tragic and shameful chapters of American history.

One of the key players in this horrific drama happened to be a zealous judge by the name of John Hathorne, a man who had little pity or mercy in his soul for the likes of those who were brought before him on charges of witchcraft. Appointed Chief Examiner of the witch trials, Hathorne was widely regarded as a cruel man, one who had already decided upon the guilt of the accused before they ever stepped foot before his bench. It speaks clearly of his character that, in the aftermath of the Salem witch trials, many of those who had taken part—whether willingly or not—offered up apologies and expressed remorse for what they had done. John Hathorne remained stubbornly unrepentant. Admittedly, some of Judge Hathorne's negative image comes from his less than sympathetic portrayal in Arthur Miller's play *The Crucible,* but even a cursory read of the Salem witch trial documents show that fiction did not fall far off the mark.

John Hathorne was the landowner of the hill in Salem Village that also bore his name, and built his home upon it in 1646. The Salem witches were executed upon the appropriately named Gallows Hill, and though Hathorne Hill is not actually Gallows Hill, what *is* known for sure is that the site of John Hathorne's old house would be the very same ground upon which a haunted hospital would be built in later years: the Danvers State Hospital.

This $1.5 million hospital for the mentally ill took four years to build, finally opening its doors to receive new patients in 1878. Males and females each had their own dedicated wing of the asylum, and if a prisoner was considered to be severely disturbed—for which we can read "potentially violent or dangerous to themselves or others"—they were placed into the care of an especially dedicated wing.

The Danvers State Asylum was sufficiently big to merit its own dedicated power station to supply all of its electrical needs. Water was drafted in from a nearby pond. As the years passed, the complex grew in size—both above ground, and also below. A massive network of underground tunnels linked up most of the buildings, built on a "spoke and wheel" design layout (picture a cart wheel in your head), with the central hub being the main administration building known as the Kirkbride building. The Kirkbride style of architecture (named after the renowned and highly respected psychiatrist Thomas Kirkbride) was extremely popular during the late 19th century, and many American insane asylums were built along similar lines—each wing was offset from its neighbor so that the residents got plenty of sunlight and fresh air, or so the theory went. The dank and cold tunnel network that interconnected these wings and accessory buildings was intended to keep the asylum functioning when the heavy snows of winter started to fall, potentially cutting Danvers State off from the outside world. Food, laundry, and the necessities of institutionalized life could all still be delivered underground.

The profession of mental health care reached a crisis point during the Depression era. Kirkbride facilities such as Danvers State were designed and built to accommodate no more than 500 to 600 patients, stretching to 700 at a pinch. But as the influx of mental patients showed no signs of slowing down, more than *2,000* were crammed into the cramped confines of this Massachusetts asylum. In what became an all too common story, the limited number of staff was simply unable to cope effectively with the sheer volume of overcrowding that was taking place. Stories of horrible "experimental" surgeries and other treatments lent the place an air of fear, so much so that author H.P. Lovecraft supposedly used Danvers State as his inspiration for the infamous Arkham Sanatorium in his horror fiction Cthulhu mythos.

Paranormal phenomena that spans the entire spectrum of activity has been reported at Danvers State over the course of its lifetime as a mental asylum; consider the apparition of a mature lady witnessed by the children of the hospital administrator in the attic of their home, for example. One of those children went on to suffer the terrifying experience of witnessing the sheets and comforter being dragged forcefully from her bed by some unseen force.

Doors throughout the asylum complex were seen to open and close, seemingly of their own accord. When Danvers State was abandoned, passers-by reported flickering lights in the vacant windows—though whether genuinely paranormal in nature, or caused by the multitude of ghost hunting teams that descended on the place, is impossible to say. Harder to explain are the accounts of disembodied footsteps, echoing through the building with no living person around to make them. While phantom footsteps are chilling enough, of even greater concern are the shouts, wails, and screams that have been heard issuing from thin air within the long-abandoned basements and tunnels at Danvers—perhaps a ghostly echo of the misery that once pervaded the asylum.

Nor were the remains of Danvers State Hospital without their ghostly apparitions. The most common sightings involved spectral patients, who have been witnessed both inside the building and walking through the grounds outside. Local folklore has it that the faces of some of the asylum's poor, tormented souls are sometimes seen peering out from the windows of certain haunted rooms.

As a paranormal investigator with 30 years of experience investigating with The Rhode Island Paranormal Research Society under his belt, Andy Laird had witnessed some incredible sights when called in to investigate a haunting. "Our investigations involved everything from the ridiculous to things nightmares are made of," Andy says, "from debunking 'paranormal activity' as actually being everyday human experience, to the rare but extreme state of demonic possession."

Although Andy officially retired from the field of paranormal investigation in 2013, he looks back upon the genesis of The Rhode Island Paranormal Research Society (and its inextricable association with Danvers State Hospital) with absolute clarity. This isn't only because of the memorable date (September 11, 1984), but because the whole thing began as the result of a bet. Andy takes up the story:

> The Rhode Island Paranormal Research Society was founded on September 11, 1984, as the result of a wager between myself and three others. We were all college students and, except for myself at that time, highly interested in researching/investigating paranormal activity. This was long before the days when such activities was even close to being

acceptable and were among a long list of social taboos. I was a hard core disbeliever in such things.

On September 10th, my friends Ray, Brenda, Tammy, and Bob and I got into a heated but friendly debate regarding ghosts. The debate resulted in a wager that either they would prove to me the existence of ghosts or they would not bring up the subject again: bring me to a place that was truly haunted. In other words, put up or shut up. The winner of the bet, officially being between Ray and I, would receive a case of Budweiser. Ray and the others looked at each other and said they knew of a place and were planning on going there that evening.

An hour later we were on the grounds of the officially closed asylum and talking to a friend of Ray's, a security guard there. After parking Ray's beat up Nova out of sight, Ray's friend opened the side door to a building that once housed the Excitable Wards.

I was creeped out just being in the powerless building and had an unshakable feeling of oppression the moment I stepped through the door. The building had been among the first to be decommissioned a while back. Paint and plaster chips riddled the floor, making our steps crackle with every step. Ray motioned for me to follow him up the stairwell while Tammy, Brenda, and Bob parted ways.

Ray and I ended up on the second floor where a heavy steel and wire door was partly open. In the hallway were rooms/cells, some with their padded doors open every 10 or so feet down the entire length of the hallway.

It had seemed like hours had passed when I observed an older man dressed in white patient's attire walk out of the cell three doors down on our left. The man suddenly stopped mid-stride, looked at me and then walked into a cell to my right, barely making it by the room's door.

I said, laughing out loud, "You're kidding me, right?"

"What the [bleep] are you talking about?" Ray replied.

I ran to the doorway and opened the door, fully expecting to find Ray's "ghost" and declare myself the winner of the wager. What I found was an empty cell and the man nowhere to be found. There was only one way in or out and nowhere to hide inside. The room was freezing cold in stark contrast to the very warm, even humid air in the hallway just feet away.

Ray stood in the doorway, looking at me very much genuinely confused by how I was acting. He denied seeing anything but me suddenly wigging out. It was then that it hit me; unlike ours, the man's footsteps didn't make any crackle or any other sound whatsoever.

On the way back home my friends wanted to hear all about my experience, but they eventually respected my being disturbed by it all, and let it be. Back home I eagerly shared the spoils of the bet and within a few hours The Rhode Island Paranormal Research Group was born, and a hardcore disbeliever was now a just as passionate a believer!

When we consider that the apparition of the patient looked directly at Andy, it seems that he encountered an intelligent haunting—one that was aware of his presence, being something more than a simple recording or imprint of a long-dead patient's image upon the atmosphere of the building.

Andy and his team went on to investigate the entire complex at Danvers—not only the buildings still left standing above ground, but also the maze of tunnels that burrow through the earth beneath them. The phenomena that they encountered there included team members being shoved by an unseen force, team members followed by the echoing footsteps of an invisible stalker, and recording sounds of crying and even some rather angry threats on their tape recorders. Andy cites the crematorium as being one of the most active hotspots in the entire facility.

"There are some places that, despite the activities of organizations seen on so-called reality television, are meant to be left alone," Andy Laird concludes. "The psychiatric hospital once located in Danvers, Massachusetts, was absolutely one of those places. It was a place that took a chilling hold of you and, all too often, demanded a high price for the intrusion."

He continued, "Having witnessed this first-hand, I often still refer to the Danvers Lunatic Asylum as a place that embodied the spider and the fly scenario. Never mind the buildings that made up the psychiatric hospital's complex, just entering the grounds was enough to give you that ominous chill of warning to smarten up and leave!"

As the years turned into decades, the funding for Danvers State Hospital started to dry up. One by one, like dominoes falling, the hospital administrators were forced to begin cutting back on beds and systematically closing down wards. By 1992, the final patients were gone and moved to other institutions across the state. Danvers State was abandoned, its hallways and rooms deserted and dark, left to slowly fade away.

The 2001 horror movie *Session 9* would be filmed in and around Danvers, making effective use of the abandoned old asylum as the backdrop for a tale of psychological terror. Danvers would also serve as the inspiration for video games and novels, all with a distinctly spooky or macabre flavor. As its haunted reputation began to grow, the location began to attract other groups of paranormal researchers.

One such investigator who has wandered the interior of Danvers in search of answers is one of the stars of the SyFy Channel's paranormal show *Haunted Collector,* Brian J. Cano. Brian was working with his team from the show *SCARED!* when I interviewed him in preparation for writing this book. I asked Brian what it actually felt like to walk those halls and tunnels. Was there an atmosphere—some remnant of the pain and misery that had been so prevalent at Danvers during its operational lifetime? Or were things calm and peaceful?

"With any such place, one goes into it with an expectation—the locale is not unknown, it is the site of pain, confusion and suffering and death. Could it be that we brought those feelings with us? Yes. Perhaps we picked up on remnants of its former inhabitants. Perhaps it was both. The place was very quiet though. That being said, perhaps that allowed our own feelings about being there to dominate."

Danvers was coming apart at the seams at the time of their visit, crumbling and rotting away. Brian and his colleagues were wary of the gaping holes in the ceilings and floorboards, treading carefully on the creaking wooden staircases as they made their way slowly into the building. Many of the rooms were in a state of near-collapse.

"We came prepared—there were no close calls, but on every floor and in every room we had to be wary," says Brian. "As the night went on, we got tired...it became harder to avoid danger spots. I'd say we were very lucky to have come out unscathed."[1]

Nonetheless, things only became truly concerning once the crew tried to leave. It is a common practice of urban explorers to identify the rooms and corridors that they have been past, using a piece of chalk to mark the doors and walls with a cross or some other easily recognizable symbol. The *SCARED!* crew were no exception, leaving a trail of chalk in their wake like a lifeline, something that could be easily followed when it came time for the weary group to backtrack.

"The place was a maze and all the floors and hallways resembled each other. As our fatigue grew, so did our disorientation. In a place like that, chalk is part of Urban Exploration 101. But despite that, we still got lost on the way out. It seemed like our chalk was being removed from some key intersections. By whom, we never knew..."

Is there a rational explanation for the chalk disappearing? Short of there being an intruder in the building, I am hard-pressed to think of one that makes any sense, and neither can Brian. But another phenomenon that might at first seem quite creepy actually has a perfectly natural cause. Odd pockets of heat seemed to pop up frequently inside the old Danvers State Hospital, at one point following Brian and his team on their journey. A viewer of the show suggested that structural decay was causing a slow release and accumulation of gases inside the old building, and that as Brian's team was moving throughout the place, the subsequently circulating air currents would carry the warmer gas pockets along with them.

As the former hospital site became increasingly dilapidated, the next step was depressingly inevitable—demolition. Despite the best efforts of those who wished to save the historic location (the building was added to the National Register of Historic Places) the wrecking balls soon began to batter the brick walls to the ground. Apartment buildings were constructed on the site, but they were gutted by a massive overnight fire that took hold in 2007. The Internet is awash with photographs of the inferno, which could be seen from many miles away.

In the aftermath of the fire, the Luxury apartments were rebuilt, and at the time of this writing still stand on the site of the old Danvers State Hospital. The façade of the once-mighty main Kirkbride building still remains, having been given a significant facelift during the renovation process. But unbeknownst to most people, there is another remnant of the days when Danvers was a functioning mental institution, hidden away behind the trees on the perimeter of the apartment complex: a cemetery.

The Danvers State Insane Asylum during the process of demolition. Photo courtesy of Devlin Mannle, Wikimedia Commons, public domain.

The human remains of several hundred (without excavating, it's impossible to tell exactly *how* many) former patients of Danvers State lie at rest in a burial ground that is tucked discreetly out of sight and out of mind of the current inhabitants. Each and every inhabitant buried there was certified insane by the State of Massachusetts. Many of the graves bear no name at all, simply an anonymous-looking marker inscribed with a number.

One hopes that the tormented souls who resided within the brick walls of the Danvers State Hospital, whether they happened to be genuinely insane or were unjustly locked away from the eyes of everyday society, have now finally found peace.

Was the Danvers State Hospital genuinely one of the world's most haunted hospitals? I put this question to Brian J. Cano.

It's my assertion that everywhere is haunted. Everything is energy—we are energy—and that which remains is everywhere. Certain places have a higher concentration of this energy and those are the places considered to be, "haunted." The events that occurred on the land before and during the tenure of the institution have added to that energy. I've gotten many reports from existing residents of the condos that strange things happen and I believe it is due to all that amassed energy...[2]

Grace Hospital
Calgary, Canada

L ocated in the southern part of the province of Alberta where two rivers come together, the city of Calgary has grown from a small 19th century settlement into a bustling 21st century metropolis that is home to well over a million Canadians. This is in no small part due to the key role played by the city in the oil and gas industries, both of which it possesses in abundance. Attracting millions of tourists each year, Calgary is a bustling hub of the arts, commerce, and higher education.

Grace Hospital was one of several hospitals that served the healthcare needs of Calgary's citizens. Rumors began to circulate about one of the second-floor obstetrics rooms (used for the delivery of babies) being haunted. According to a story that is still making the rounds today, the apparition of a mournful woman cradling a ghostly child in her arms would often be seen in that particular labor and delivery room. This is the restless spirit of a mother who died in childbirth along with her child, and is known for opening windows and banging noisily on walls and pipes.

Any mother going into labor in the haunted room would suffer the most dreadfully complicated birth, or so the story goes, requiring an obstetrician to remove the baby by Caesarian section. The land on which Grace Hospital was built was once the homestead of this young lady's family; she died while giving birth in one of the rooms of that original house, and lingers after her death out of the fear that other young women delivering babies in what used to be her room will meet the same tragic fate as she once did. And yet, still other reports claim that the ghost could be that of a nurse.

This is where fact and fantasy have merged, combining into a tale that is a curious mix of truth and fiction.

To this day, the ghost is still claimed by some to be that of a philanthropist named Maudine (also known as Maude) Riley, a schoolteacher who was also a pillar of the community in her day. Maude was a highly influential figure in the area of nurturing and protecting children, founding the Calgary Childhood Welfare Society in 1918. Researcher John Savoie has put together a biography of this extraordinary lady, and found that she was a member of no less than 30 organizations devoted to the betterment of her fellow human beings—though the care of children always remained closest to her heart.[1]

"Children should be well born, well treated, well housed, well fed, and well taught," she was known to say. And by all contemporary accounts, Maude lived this credo every day of her life, working tirelessly in pursuit of her goal: to enrich the lives of disadvantaged children. One possible reason for her fierce drive is that one of

Maude's three pregnancies was a touch-and-go affair, very nearly killing her and her child in the process. It has been speculated that Maude's burning desire to protect children and mothers originated with this difficult birth.

And therein lies the first major problem with the tale, and the reason why the ghostly mother at Grace Hospital cannot be Maude Riley—because Maude Riley *never* died in childbirth. She in fact went on to live to a respectable old age, surviving until the year 1962. She would have been far too old to be the ghostly mother who haunted the delivery room.

Like all good stories, this one contains more than a grain of truth. What was once the maternity ward at Grace Hospital has since become part of a health resource center, known as the Riley Park Health Centre. "...the newly renovated third floor at Calgary's old Grace Hospital is positively comfy," wrote author Richard Cairney in the *Canadian Medical Association Journal* in 1998, soon after its renovation. "It's soothing colour schemes, oak and brass trim, and carpeted floors complement 3 state-of-the-art operating rooms, 37 beds, 8 day-surgery beds and 6 postop recovery beds.

"All of this makes the Health Resources Centre look like the hospital of your dreams. It comes with many more creature comforts than the old Grace, whose cold marble mouldings and harsh fluorescent lights are testament to a time when hospitals were indeed cold, harsh institutions."[2]

The Riley Park Health Center is so named because of the park situated across the street from it, which *is* named after the Riley family, who donated it to the city of Calgary in 1904. They graciously provided the land on which Grace Hospital would later be built, but we must look elsewhere for the identity of the mysterious maternal ghost.

PSICAN—Paranormal Studies and Investigations Canada— collects accounts of hauntings and other paranormal activity, including the ghostly goings-on at both the old Grace Hospital and the newer Riley Park Health Centre that went on to replace it.

One security guard told PSICAN of his early experiences at Grace during the mid-1990s. Although the second floor was shut down at the time, the first and third floors still contained patients. Other security guards and the nursing staff had warned him about the ghostly activity that took place in the hospital, but he paid it little heed.

The guard made a habit of heading up to the now-abandoned maternity floor and watching one of his favorite TV shows in the patient lounge up there, pulling up a chair to catch the latest installment of *Star Trek: Voyager*. After the show, he would put the chair back in its place, turn the TV off, and resume his patrol of the hospital.

Only the guard and the building engineer had keys to gain access to the locked-up second floor. Patrolling the old maternity ward, he was suddenly overcome with a smell that was all-too familiar. "I recognized it because my wife a year earlier while driving her to the hospital (she was pregnant), her water broke in our car. And I remembered it as the same smell of embryonic fluid. But in my head, I knew that there were no more births performed here and it had been months since we had locked up the floor."

Making his way back to the TV room, the security guard must have been more than a little disconcerted to hear voices. Walking in, he found that the TV was back on, and the chair that he had put away was sitting squarely in front of it once more. Except, he had not done it. And nobody else was up on the deserted second floor.

Calling his backup security partner, the guard was told that the building engineer was down in the basement working on something and had not been up there to the second. The second guard did not have a set of master keys either. Perhaps, the second guard suggested, the ghosts were playing a game with him?

It wasn't long before the mysterious prankster struck again. Summoned back to the security desk by his partner, the guard was less than happy to see that a "call security" alarm was summoning him to Operating Room #2. On inspection of the operating room, the guard found that the "call security" button had been physically pushed in, something that no mere mechanical failure could explain away. Electrical short circuits might be a reasonable explanation, until one considers the fact that electricity shorting is incapable of actually pushing in a button. Resetting it, the guard went back to the security desk.

He made it only partway back before his radio crackled into life with another "call security" alarm, this time coming from Operating Room #1. The guard ran, presumably hoping to catch this practical joker in the act. But arriving in Operating Room #1, he found the call button depressed and no signs of life anywhere.

Perhaps it was a coincidence that both operating rooms were located directly across the hallway from the TV room?

"Look…" the guard began hesitantly, addressing the thin air. "I know you might feel lonely, as all the mothers and babies are gone now. And I'm sorry that you feel this way. But I have a job to do. My job is to take care of this place and keep it safe. So I'm asking you, pleeeease…don't keep calling us up here. We need to do our jobs. Thank you, and amen."

Needless to say, the security guards were never again bothered by ghostly activity after that.

"I never seen a ghost there," the guard concluded. "Only what I've testified above. I will say, that hospital does have many eyes, as I never felt alone in it. Like I was always being watched, no matter where I went."

Could the "call security" alarm-pusher have perhaps been the sad and lonely maternal spirit seen by multiple staff and patients on the maternity floor, desperate for company now that the constant flow of expectant mothers and newborn babies had stopped?

All that we can say for certain is...*somebody* had to have been pushing those buttons.

Just because the old hospital was closed down, replaced with a newer, more modern facility in the form of a health resource center does not mean that the ghosts went away. In fact quite the opposite is the case, if the account of a patient undergoing back surgery there is to be believed.

Turning to walk back into their room (the gender of this particular patient is not known) the patient was surprised to find the figure of a dark-haired woman sitting in one of the chairs. Based upon her white uniform, the patient quite reasonably assumed that it was a member of the nursing staff. Flustered, the patient looked back an instant later, only to find that the nurse had disappeared.

The patient went on to have a restless night, disturbed by the nagging feeling of the mysterious nurse constantly returning to the room. Not only did it seem that somebody invisible were sitting on the bed with them, but the patient also experienced the disconcerting sensation of an invisible touch on their skin throughout the night.

It wasn't until the following morning, hearing the nurses talk about the phantom sister reputed to haunt that particular part of the building, that the patient put two and two together. In this case, the story held that the nurse roamed the halls of the hospital in search of the baby that she had lost at childbirth, as she had died while in the process of delivering it. The flesh-and-blood nurses on the ward were quick to blame lost items and equipment on their ghostly colleague.

"I did not tell anybody because I was still trying to process it," the patient reported to PSICAN. "I absolutely saw a lady in my room and she was gone seconds later. I definitely felt somebody sitting on my bed and I had my eyes open. This was a real experience and I remember it vividly."

The mystery of the ghost on the second floor's identity may never be solved, but we have no reason to believe that she has stopped walking the floor just yet....

CHAPTER 14

Metropolitan State Hospital
Waltham, Massachusetts, USA

O nce a paragon of all that was the best and brightest in the field of mental health care, the formidable edifice of Massachusetts's Metropolitan State Hospital has since been reduced by time, weather, and circumstance, to a shell of its former glory. Its Colonial-style buildings have mostly fallen into disrepair and are virtually ruins. Following its closure in 1992, the powers-that-be decided to knock down most of the facility buildings, although the boarded-up main administration building still stands as a poignant reminder of the many lives spent within the old hospital's red brick walls. Weeds and wild plant life dominate the site today.

Things were completely different when the hospital first opened its doors during the late 1920s. Metropolitan State was intended to be a cutting-edge facility at the time, playing a leading role in the care of Massachusetts's mentally ill patient population. This wasn't just restricted to adult patients—a sub-facility named The Gaebler Children's Center was built in 1955, intended to serve the mental healthcare needs of children as young as 6 years old (upon reaching the age of 18, patients would be relocated to Metropolitan State itself). The campus sprawled not only above ground, but also beneath; a subterranean network of tunnels connected the multiple treatment wards, accommodation buildings for employees and medical staff, and the multitude of other facilities necessary to support a thousand patients—not least of which being an on-site morgue.

Sadly, Metropolitan State Hospital somehow got caught in a downward spiral of terrible conditions, patient neglect, and sometimes outright abuse. Former patients (including some who were children at the time) have gone on record to speak about their experiences of being left naked and alone in isolation rooms.[1] Whereas the crowded patient wards were stiflingly hot with virtually no airflow (most windows were permanently locked) the hospital staff enjoyed the luxury of air conditioning in their areas. It was by no means a safe and comfortable place to be, let alone a true house of healing.

As a young legislator, future Massachusetts governor and United States presidential candidate Michael Dukakis visited the neighboring Fernald Center. In a later interview, he went on to describe it as an unbelievable experience, and one that he would never forget.

Although many of the patients housed at Metropolitan State were regarded as essentially harmless, others were decidedly less so. Take, for example, the strange and disturbing case of Melvin Wilson, who spent nearly 40 years of his life as a patient in mental institutions. A 36-six year-old patient by the name of Ann Marie Davee had disappeared, seemingly without a trace, in 1978. Rather disconcertingly, Ann Marie's vanishing seemed to ruffle very few feathers among the hospital staff. Indeed, a serious investigation wasn't even contemplated until the following year, spurred on by a series of complaints regarding unexplained patient deaths at state medical facilities, which finally caused the Massachusetts senate to intervene.

When a search was finally made, seven of Anne Marie's teeth were found in Melvin's possession—as was the hatchet that police investigators believed he had used to chop her body into several pieces. As a 1980 *St. Joseph Gazette* tells the story: "Investigators on Tuesday discovered the body of Ann Marie Davee, who was 36 when she disappeared from Metropolitan State Hospital in 1978, buried in 'three or four holes,' at the mental institution, said Kenneth Wayne, an attorney general's spokesman."[2]

Two years passed from the time of Ann Marie's dismemberment at Melvin's hands until the discovery of multiple body parts. Her killer was hurriedly relocated to the Bridgewater State Hospital, a facility that was much better equipped to handle such violent and homicidal patients as Melvin. Apart from his being mentally disturbed, any other reasons that Melvin might have had for murdering his fellow patient have never come to light.

Although Metropolitan State isn't well-known globally, numerous would-be ghost hunters still find their way to the site. An appearance on the TV show *The Scariest Places on Earth* (fronted by none other than *The Exorcist* star Linda Blair) helped cement the hospital's reputation. With her distinctively creepy voice, actress Zelda Rubinstein (best known for portraying the psychic medium Tangina in the movie *Poltergeist*) describes the hospital as being somewhere with a "history so grim, the exact location cannot be revealed."

"It was worse than a mental ward," states a former security guard during an on-camera interview. "It was like Hell...Hell on

Earth." The remainder of the episode segment features a group of first-time urban explorers, who enter the old hospital armed only with flashlights and proceed to discover the desiccated remains of long-dead animals and a generally decaying interior. Making their way toward what was once the hospital morgue, one of the male team members is suddenly spooked by something that he sees in the dark, and causes the entire group to flee. That *something,* he tells his fellows explorers afterward, was a human leg belonging to nobody else in the group—a leg that he could see moving in the dark.

SyFy has posted the segment on Youtube, and I encourage you to watch the video and take a look at Metropolitan State Hospital (both the inside and the outside) for yourself.[3]

If they should choose to hike through the woods that surround it, following a leafy nature trail along Trapelo Road, those who visit the site of the former Metropolitan State Hospital may happen upon its cemetery, the last resting place for many of the old hospital's patients between the years of 1947 and 1979—approximately 310 souls, according to the sign that stands at the entrance. Known as the Metfern Cemetery (due to its shared tenancy with the neighboring Fernald School for the developmentally disabled, whose reputation for harsh living conditions rivalled that of Metropolitan State) this burial ground is usually overgrown and not all that easy to find. The letters "C" and "P" inscribed on each tombstone identify whether the person interred beneath it was a member of the Catholic or the Protestant faith.

Blogger Shuko Tamao visited the cemetery on a sunny October day in 2010, and found it to be a fascinating experience:

An altar roughly divides the Catholic and Protestant plots. My husband, Brian, was following after me while I was investigating the cemetery. As I returned from the Protestant side, he was looking at a gravestone of an Irish baby girl. He seemed to be feeling closer to her because she was born only a year different from him. Considering from her young age, she might have been at Fernald.

There was a new cross in front of the altar, contributed by the ex-children of the Gaebler (the Metropolitan State Hospital for youths). They must have visited the Gaebler building before the demolition, and then stopped by the graveyard with the cross. We all should remember a thoughtful note from them: "Though your names are not known, Your lives will never be forgotten..."[4]

Visiting the site of Metropolitan State on an April day in 2013, Laura Giuliano and her fellow paranormal investigators from Para-Boston started out by visiting the building that once went by the

Ruins at Metropolitan State and the Metfern Cemetery. Photo courtesy of Laura Giuliano.

name of Kline Hall, but today serves as the home for a community access cable station, along with some administrative offices, a fitness center, and an auditorium.

Her team recorded the eerie sounds of children at play inside the premises, humming and singing. One claim that is commonly made regarding Metropolitan State is that a physician supposedly caused the accidental deaths of up to 12 children in that building, poisoning them with strontium-laced milk. Although the doctor's motives are believed to have been good—the hope was that administering strontium would effectively treat the children's mental illnesses—the outcome was both fatal and tragic. This is why the spirits of these dead children supposedly haunt the hospital to this day.

I have been unable to verify the truth of this particular story, and so, intriguing though it may sound, it has to be placed in the category of folklore unless actual evidence comes to light. However, that is not the only urban legend associated with the old hospital; that classic tale of the hospital being built on a Native American burial ground is also told in conjunction with Metropolitan State, as with so many other reputedly haunted places in the United States.

Laura Giuliano's visit left a deep impression upon her, and she remembers the experience clearly to this day:

Having spent the last 20 years living within a few short miles of Metropolitan State, and having heard rumors of its history and alleged hauntings, the hospital has always been a special place of intrigue and mystery for me. For years, security vans were always parked by the entrance and I would fantasize about slipping by them and exploring the grounds and buildings. After most of the buildings and underground tunnels were demolished, the vans were gone, the "No Trespassing" signs were removed, and what was left of Metropolitan State was free to be explored.

The land is more than an expanse of grass, dirt roads, and paved roads leading to nowhere and an abandoned building still standing watch over it all. The grounds feel as though they have a soul to them and the feeling of sadness in the air of the lives that have lived there is almost palpable. There is a certain eerie feeling as you slowly walk toward the most visible building that remains—the Administration Building. It's a stately brick building that must have been quite imposing back in the day. Now it has crumbling brick, flaking paint, boarded windows, and the weeds have long since begun to blanket its walls. Upon closer approach, various pieces of stray litter lay near the foundation and, upon closer examination, are hospital items—alcohol wipes, hospital paperwork, part of an old stethoscope, etc.

After further exploring the grounds and the woods that encircle it, I stumbled upon an area in the woods not far from the main road. Having been early Spring, the trees were still barren and a shiny object caught my eye deeper into the woods perhaps 100 feet in. As I walked towards this glitter, another more ominous feeling overcame me but I had no idea why. I noticed there were slight solid stairs in the ground as I came closer to the object that caught my eye. I wondered how long ago the last person had walked these stairs as each of my feet ascended. There were still the ruins of a small shack-like structure. The more I looked around, the more I saw old rusty pieces of something. Poison Ivy was covering much of this 10' x 10' spot so I used a long branch to further poke around. Soon I found a women's leather shoe and I wondered what on Earth this area was. The closest thing I could imagine was that it was an old campsite. Then my branch snagged on something—at first it looked like an old, dirty white shirt. I lay down the stick and tugged on this "shirt" to unearth it and it proved to be far bigger than I had imagined. I saw some writing and brushed off the dirt and read "Metropolitan State Hospital." The finding gave me a kind of sick, lonely feeling at the pit of my stomach, but I wasn't sure why. I ripped off that section of what turned out to be a bed sheet and I continued to explore other areas of the forest.

I stumbled upon Metfern Cemetery. There were rumors that old graves had been dug up and moved to an area in the woods. This cemetery would have been just a sad cemetery because of the story of moving the remains of past patients and the anonymous grave markings of letters and numbers, but the day I was there I saw something more troubling. One

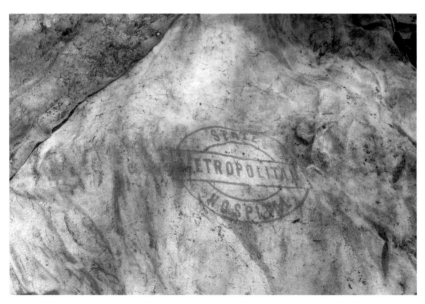

An old Metropolitan State bedsheet found by investigators on the grounds.
Photo courtesy of Laura Giuliano.

of the graves had been recently dug up and a deep hole was all that remained.

Intrigued by so many eerie feelings and the mystery of stories that would never be told, I arranged for my paranormal investigation team, Para-Boston, to hold an investigation in another building that still remains from the old Metropolitan State Hospital. It was then, upon doing research about the site, that I learned of the murder of Ann Marie Davee by fellow patient Melvin Wilson. I read there was a "hut" in the woods where the two of them would meet and their clothes and sheets were found there after Miss Davee's disappearance. My heart jumped into my stomach and I wondered if I had just uncovered the exact spot where a brutal murder had taken place in 1978. Was I the only one who now knew of this location, long since overgrown by weeds and brush? Was I Ann Marie's last link to the living remembering where she took her last breath and caring that she had lived her life at all?

Apartment buildings have recently been built on the property, just a stone's throw from where the old hospital buildings once stood. Travel writer J.W. Ocker visited the building in 2013, writing about it on his blog "Odd Things I've Seen."

The building is located on Metropolitan Parkway South and is pretty hard to miss. The red brick edifice and its glaring, flaking white portico looms more than two stories above a relatively blank area, a strange combination of out in the middle of nowhere and right in the middle of everything. No buildings are directly around it, but there is an entire apartment complex almost within jumping distance. One side is bordered by forest and a rutted asphalt street encircles the building, so you can easily see it from all sides.

The exterior lives up to everything you expect from an abandoned building. The windows are boarded and bricked up, the walls are overgrown with clinging plants, the lawn is hairy with tall weeds, a sign tacked to one wall frantically warns about asbestos and cancer. Surprisingly and refreshingly, there was only a minimum amount of graffiti, just a few simple scrawlings on the front door area, including the word "Welcome" on the doorstep.

The building still bears its name, the Dr. William F. McLaughlin building (named after a WWII flight surgeon who became a hospital administrator there) high up on the roof of the portico, just under the white-washed Great Seal of the Commonwealth of Massachusetts, with its Native American figure beneath a bodiless arm brandishing a sword in his direction and a Latin motto about peace by that same weapon surrounding it all.

At the time that I visited, I didn't know about the Davee murder, but thinking back, the place looked like it could have been absolutely paved with the shallow graves of severed body parts.[5]

With the history of pain, fear, and the entire gamut of negative emotions that took place inside mental health facilities such as Metropolitan State, it should come as no surprise that the stories of ghostly activity would follow. Shadow figures were frequently reported inside the hospital buildings, even when the facility was still an active health care institution.

Unlike many of the haunted hospitals that we have learned about in this book, the reader is still able to access some of the grounds of Metropolitan State without too many problems. Although the few buildings left standing are sealed off for reasons of personal safety (asbestos has been found throughout the interior), at the time of writing, prospective visitors are still permitted to stroll through the trees and grasslands surrounding the administrative building.

If you should find yourself in the area, why not visit the grounds one evening at sundown and take a few moments to let the sense of history surrounding the crumbling old house of healing make itself felt. After all, who knows what else might make its presence felt....

The Old Changi Hospital
Singapore

I t is commonly accepted that some buildings become haunted simply because of all the pain, misery, and suffering that was inflicted upon the helpless souls who once resided there. Arguably the single greatest cause of such negative emotion is the scourge that has plagued humanity ever since the first human picked up a rock and hit another over the head with it: war.

The British armed forces maintained a significant presence in Singapore during the 1930s. Although the British Empire was a true global power in every sense of the phrase—as the popular saying went at the time, "The sun never sets upon the British Empire"— an ominous red sun was slowly rising in the east to challenge its supremacy. The empire of Japan was furiously expanding its army, navy, and air force, casting an avaricious eye toward Great Britain's Pacific holdings.

Recognizing this growing threat, the British government began to slowly but surely reinforce its military bases throughout Asia. A steady stream of soldiers, sailors, airmen, and marines traded in the gloomy grey skies of Great Britain for the scorching hot climes of such defensive bastions such as Singapore, which was one of the key strategic naval bases in that region.

The Japanese Navy launched a sneak dawn attack upon the American Pacific fleet at Pearl Harbor early on the Sunday morning of December 7, 1941, which would be known forever as "A day that will live in infamy." On the following day, Japanese amphibious forces invaded Malaya, either sweeping aside or firmly crushing all resistance. The British forces were both outflanked and outfought by their opponents, driven back time and time again, until they were finally forced to retreat upon their stronghold at Singapore. Adding further insult to injury, the pride of the Royal Navy—the battleship HMS *Prince of Wales* and her escorting ships—was pulverized by Japanese air power.

By February of 1942, Japanese soldiers were marching triumphantly through the streets of Singapore. In what British Prime Minister Winston Churchill would later to refer to as the worst capitulation in British military history, somewhere around 160,000 British and Allied troops (records are still incomplete today) were captured by the invading Japanese army. Many would meet a horrific fate at the hands of their captors, such as those patients who were convalescing at Singapore's primary hospital, the Alexandra Military Hospital, and were stabbed to death while still laying helplessly in their sick beds. Some were even butchered upon the operating tables, as crazed Japanese soldiers burst into the theaters while the British surgical teams were still going about their life-saving work.

Panoramic view of the front courtyard at Changi. Photo courtesy of Kelvin Tan, 360 Snapshots.

Despite this sickening atrocity, which history has now named "The Alexandra Hospital Massacre," the hospital did not develop a reputation for being greatly haunted (though it does have its ghost stories). That questionable accolade was bestowed instead upon the much smaller Royal Air Force Hospital at Changi, which was a barracks block for soldiers at the time Singapore fell, in addition to playing a medical role. Although we have no records of a massacre taking place there, the facility *was* used as a makeshift holding camp for British and allied prisoners of war held during the Japanese occupation, as well as dissident Singaporeans—locals whom the Japanese believed were hostile to the occupation of their homeland.

Based upon prisoner accounts, conditions there were grim, with overcrowding and poor hygiene an accepted part of everyday life. Perhaps worst of all, the Japanese secret police (an organization known as the *Kempeitai* and run along very similar lines to that of the Nazi Gestapo) used the barracks as a place of interrogation and outright torture. The walls echoed day and night to the piteous screams of brutalized men when the Kempeitai interrogators plied their vicious trade. And as we will find out shortly when we look at the haunting of the former Changi Hospital, there is no shortage of people who claim that those same screams still echo through those very same corridors to this day.

The hospital continued to serve the healthcare needs of Changi's citizens until 1997, when a newer, larger hospital facility entered service. As the newly founded Changi General Hospital expanded and flourished, the abandoned facility that it replaced began to flounder and wither away. As with so many historic old buildings with troubled pasts, it did not take long for the ghost stories to start spreading.

A fairly typical tale associated with Changi involves five friends who went to the abandoned hospital one Saturday night. Shortly before midnight, the party made their way inside, where they were surprised by a "very loud, hacking voice about a foot to the side of us." Unsurprisingly the group bolted, fleeing the empty old building with a mix of screaming and hysterical laughter.

Another visitor by the name of Ramesh has an even more disturbing story. He visited the old Changi Hospital on several occasions in 2013, shooting video footage outside the building. But Ramesh may have brought home more than a few video files with him. He claims to have been awoken at around 3 a.m. by the disconcerting feeling of a weight or pressure bearing down upon his chest. Ramesh goes on to say that he was not only unable to breathe, but that he also felt a sensation akin to being hugged, and could hear somebody breathing in his ear.

As a medical professional, my first concern would be that he might have been experiencing some kind of heart problem. But Ramesh goes on to tell of two apparitions seen by his father: a Chinese male and female, both young in appearance, and dressed in clothing consistent with the World War II era. Ramesh believed they were the ghosts of two victims of Japanese torture—and presumably murder. Following a number of prayers, the apparitions were not seen again.[1]

Ramesh is not the only person to have apparently brought back something unexpected to their home after spending a night at the old Changi Hospital. One of Singapore's best resources for local ghost stories and folklore is the website *www.hungzai.com*, whose webmaster graciously granted me permission to share some of the stories that relate to Changi in this book. One young man experienced nothing obviously paranormal while he was inside the hospital itself (other than feeling nauseous when trying to enter one of the rooms) but things rapidly took a turn for the worse when he arrived back at his empty house. Relaxing on the bed, he was suddenly disturbed by odd noises coming from underneath it. One can only imagine how frightened he was when the bed then began to rock backward and forward, as though shaken by some unseen force. His screams were so loud that they brought the maid running from her own quarters within the grounds.[2]

Another witness had a friend who once worked as an orderly at the hospital. The orderly recalled hearing the noises of what sounded like ghostly children running around on the floors above him when he worked night shifts there. The children sounded as though they were having a great time, laughing, joking, and playing—and interestingly enough, were speaking with definite English accents. Considering that hundreds of British servicemen and women were stationed at Changi throughout the years, this is hardly surprising; many would have given birth to children during their posting to Singapore, and there are many websites with postings made by British and other Commonwealth children who were born at the old Changi Hospital before the military handed it over to the local government. It is pleasant to think that not all of the ghosts that haunt the hospital have a basis in torture and pain.

And yet, there are other accounts from those who have visited the hospital and encountered the apparitions of children who seemed far from happy. Consider the story told by a group of friends who, like so many others before them, decided to explore the abandoned old hospital building one night. Perhaps unwisely, the group broke up into pairs. As one pair headed deeper into the building, and just as they were passing the elevator shaft, they were both startled by a sound not dissimilar to the tinkling of a bell. The elevator doors began to open, despite there being no power to the building. That alone would have been enough to send most people on their way out of the building at high speed, but our intrepid duo kept on exploring. It is worth mentioning that, even when the hospital was without electrical power in most areas, a number of visitors have witnessed electrical devices such as this elevator and spinning ceiling fans, operating all by themselves.

Like the hospital orderly, this inquisitive pair experienced what seems to be the most common type of paranormal phenomena reported at the old Changi Hospital: the sound of voices originating from the old hospital wards. Auditory phenomena encountered at this particular haunted location ranges from a gentle, quiet whispering sound to blood-curdling shrieks of agony and despair, which have set more than one visitor into a panic. As if all of that wasn't chilling enough, the sound of disembodied laughter is also heard inside those walls, and sometimes closes in upon the unsuspecting intruder.

Other ghost hunters claim to have heard the sound of slippers slapping across the surfaces of the long-empty floors, the measured tread of shoes or boots stepping upon tile, and even the squeaking of the wheelchairs and wheeled gurneys that were once used to transfer patients from room to room. The noise of many marching boots on parade, responding to the shouted orders of a non-commissioned officer, have also been reported by people passing by outside—though whether these are the echoes of long-dead British or Japanese soldiers is impossible to determine.

Suddenly, as the two unauthorized nocturnal visitors moved toward the staircase, one of them stopped dead in his tracks, turned almost white in color, and then insisted that they get out of the building right away. Sensibly, they made their way back to the exit and left the old hospital to its ghosts for the rest of the evening.

What had the poor man seen that had caused him to take such fright? "A little boy, pale bluish/purplish skin, sitting at the corner, staring at him..."[3]

Many of the hospital ghost stories involve the apparitions of children, or at least what *appear* to be children. In addition to the pallid little boy in the corner, another group of visitors sighted a young girl clutching a teddy bear. This ghost seemed to be standing *on* the staircase and walking down it, advancing slowly toward them. What they found most disturbing about this particular apparition was not the blood spots on her plain white dress; it was the fact that the girl was singing the last verses of the children's song that they themselves had just finished singing: *Baa Baa Black Sheep*.[4]

Few of the apparitions seen in and around the old Changi Hospital are of the kind, peaceful variety—though one exception is the ghostly security guard who once worked there, and continues to make his rounds after death. He has been mistaken for a flesh-and-blood night watchman by more than one stared trespasser. But most of the ghosts of Changi are terrifying in appearance. For example, take the case of the nervous visitor who claimed to have seen the corridors filled with faceless shadow figures, staring down mutely at the flesh and blood people who were perhaps being perceived as invading their domain. The same man went on to describe how he and his friends were being stalked by the ghostly figure of a long-haired woman with a "sinister black aura" following their group around the hospital. He refused to describe this female apparition in any greater detail, because, he said, "...it's so horrible, you will not want to hear..."[5]

Other ghosts seen both in and around the hospital grounds and in the vicinity of the chalets located at the bottom of the hill upon which the old hospital still stands, include the disturbing apparition of an old man who seems to have been struck by a vehicle and left to die in agony at the roadside. And what are we to make of the figure seen hanging in one of the trees, with long white hair standing up on end, which caused a female paranormal thrill-seeker to not only faint dead away one night, but also to lose control of her bladder?[6] Figures in white clothing, similar to nightgowns or long white dresses, are a recurring theme in the ghost sightings at this location, and the apparition of a wheelchair-bound old lady has also been seen, staring back at the unwelcome visitor from a face that is framed by long white hair. Although more unnerving than harmful, this mournful specter has been known to follow some groups around the hospital, seemingly trailing in their wake.

Depending on your own personal set of beliefs, perhaps the most frightening entity said to reside at the old Changi Hospital is what is known to the people of Malaya and the surrounding area as a *Toyol*. In southeast Asian folklore, a Toyol is a spirit being conjured up by a witch doctor or other similar practitioner of the arcane, and is said to be derived from the remains of an aborted fetus. The Chinese, Taiwanese, Korean, and other neighboring societies all have a similar variant of the Toyol as part of their culture. They are said to be primarily creatures of annoyance, petty theft, and general mayhem, though this is belied by what sounds like a rather terrifying appearance.

Most descriptions of the Toyol sound like some sort of cross between Gollum from *The Lord of the Rings* movies and Sloth from *The Goonies*. In fact, entering the word "Toyol" into an Internet search engine brings up a range of both entertainingly schlocky and disturbing images from around the world, including a few from some truly dire-looking horror movies. In stories, the Toyol is usually described as looking like a green-skinned baby with a bulbous, overgrown head; the teeth are sharp and jagged, the ears pointed and swept back, and the eyes look distinctly inhuman.

Legend has it that most Toyols are male, the rationale being that female Toyols are supposedly harder to control because they are both more willful and more vicious than their male counterparts. Although most accounts paint them as being primarily mischievous, the Toyol has also been described as malevolent and vengeful on occasion. Although the idea of a Toyol might be difficult for us to believe in the midst of our rational 21st century scientific world, it is important to understand that a belief in such entities still runs strong in this part of the world, and shows no sign of dying off anytime soon.

Sightings of a green boy have been reported from inside the old Changi Hospital on more than one occasion. According to one account, the Toyol was seen playing with a stone, tossing it against one of the walls like a ball. This "baby ghost" appeared to be playing hide and seek with a different bunch of visitors, ducking out of sight and cautiously reappearing again from behind a different door or pillar.

The paranormal can be experienced by any of the human senses. We have already learned about the apparitions sighted at the old Changi Hospital, and of the voices and sounds of yesteryear that still echo through the now-empty rooms and corridors. Another intriguing aspect of this particular haunting is that of the unusual odors that seem to come and go without apparent cause. Visitors to the former operating theaters relate being immersed in the overwhelming stench of blood, but it is just as common for the smell of cleaning and sanitizing chemicals to appear.

Until security monitoring systems were put in place just recently, it was regarded as something of a cool and quirky pasttime for locals to head on up to the hospital at night in search of a good fright. As we have already seen, some of these "paranormal tourists" got significantly more than they had bargained for.

The old Changi Hospital now stands abandoned, the local authorities apparently unsure of what to do with it next. Plans to turn the facility into a luxury spa and resort fell through in 2009. Regular break-ins over the years have resulted in the crumbling walls being daubed with occult symbols from both Asian and western European culture such as inverted crosses and the number 666, along with other graffiti and acts of vandalism.

Several TV shows have used the hospital as a shooting location, and in 2010 a film crew spent some time there shooting a movie. *Haunted Changi* is a "found footage" mockumentary-style drama, in a similar vein to *The Blair Witch Project, REC,* and the horde of other similarly derivative movies that jumped on the bandwagon. The movie follows a small camera crew who are supposedly trying to get to the bottom of the hauntings at the old Changi Hospital, only to find (much to their surprise, but not to that of the audience) that the unquiet dead do not want to be found.

Working on a shoestring budget and shooting in a sometimes nauseating hand-held "shaky cam," the producers have made (in my opinion) a passable found footage horror movie with one or two moments that may make you jump a little. Although it isn't going to be considered for an Oscar any time soon, the movie is worth taking a look at, if for no other reason than getting a comprehensive tour of one of the world's most haunted hospitals, not only during the daylight, but also after darkness has fallen.

Slowly but surely, the old hospital has become increasingly famous for its ghostly denizens, attracting a steadily increasing number of paranormal investigators who are eager to unlock its secrets. One such man is Noel Boyd, investigator for the popular ghost-hunting show *Ghost Files Singapore*. As a young boy growing up, Noel was actually terrified of ghosts and the supernatural, but when his family actually moved into a haunted house, everything changed. "I guess it's in my nature to fight back when I'm cornered," he told me during our interview. "I started reading every article I could find on the internet about ghosts and poltergeist activities. I was hooked within days! I spoke to Buddhist mediums, Catholic priests, and paranormal investigators just so I could pick their brains."

When Noel and his friends started shooting *Ghost Files Singapore,* they had a number of promising locations that they wanted to spend the night investigating. But one property sat right at the very top of their wish list: the old Changi Hospital. The sheer volume of ghost stories that the *GFS* presenters had heard about the place bordered on ridiculous. "Every Singaporean has heard at least one OCH related ghost story. Besides being a country that is nuts about ghost stories, there is a lot of substance to these stories. I have friends that have been there at night and they will never return to the place because of their unique encounters."

What was the worst story that had come their way? "Probably the one about the demonic possession which occurred over at old Changi," Noel told me. "Luckily, the guy's friends managed to drag him out of there and carried him to a nearby temple to get him taken care of."

Quiet understandably, Noel and his ghost-hunting crew didn't take the former hospital's fearsome reputation lightly when they set about conducting an overnight investigation there one night. As the darkness continued to deepen, the *Ghost Files Singapore* team walked cautiously up to the hospital's main entrance. "The first thing I felt when I approached the building was the eerie feeling of being watched," says Noel. This is a very common theme in the testimonies of those who have spent time inside the old Changi Hospital, particularly after night has fallen. There is a definite sense of not being alone, of being in the presence of unknown, unseen observers.

Not to be spooked, the investigators began to fire off photographs of the surrounding windows and doorways. All of them appeared to be empty, but when the team reviewed their haul of digital images prior to entering the hospital, Noel was surprised to discover what he believes to be a human figure standing in one of the seemingly empty windows, staring straight back at him. Noel knew almost immediately that they were going to be in for a wild night.

Undeterred by the presence of an apparently spectral observer, the *GFS* investigators made their way inside. As soon as Noel and the boys had crossed the threshold, the atmosphere turned deathly cold. "When I took my first step into the building, I felt coldness. Singapore is a hot and humid country so that in itself was a given sign. There were times where I felt fear shoot right through my body. I had to be calm and collected no matter how I felt. Thankfully I had teammates that I could count on."

Moving slowly from room to room, the ghost hunters set about conducting an experiment with a "spirit box" or "ghost box"— an electronic tool that some people believe will allow disembodied spirits to communicate with the living. The spirit box works by constantly scanning radio frequencies, hopping from radio station to radio station, and spitting out a stream of white noise and fragments of speech and sound. Some investigators believe that the spirit box allows any entities that are present to manipulate those radio transmissions into some kind of understandable message by cherry-picking the words that make the most sense to them. Another school of thought is that the spirit box provides a technological medium for spirits to manifest their own voices, superimposing them on top of the background noise of the radio transmissions.

Use of the spirit box has always been controversial, and the device has polarized the paranormal research community to a certain degree. Whereas some paranormal investigators are true believers, claiming to have obtained the most fantastic results when using one, others discredit it entirely, using the argument that what we are really listening to is just plain gibberish. The jury is still out.

Noel and his compatriots decided they would employ it just like any other tool, and let the chips fall where they may. It wasn't to be long before they received the name "Andrew" from the device, although there was little in the way of meaningful communication. If "Andrew" was actually real (and getting an English name in a former Royal Air Force hospital makes sense) then he wasn't feeling particularly talkative. Could "Andrew" have been the watcher by the window? Or was he nothing more than a fragment from a local radio station's evening broadcast?

"Till this day I don't know if we are communicating with spirits or a demonic entity," says Noel. "It boggles my mind all the time. I read an interview with a Catholic priest who said demons sometimes pretend to be ghosts so that they can communicate with paranormal investigators. Whatever it is, that entity we communicated with called itself Andrew. And hey, Andrew was nice so maybe it wasn't demonic."

As the *Ghost Files Singapore* investigators stalked their way through the hospital complex, things were relatively calm and quiet until they passed what was once the canteen and food service area, when a disembodied groaning noise startled them. They also heard what sounded like shoes on the concrete floor—women's high heels was the impression that Noel got—after which everything went quiet. Readings on the handheld EMF meters dropped to minimal levels and stayed there. When I asked Noel about his theory concerning this sudden drop in activity, he told me, "On hindsight, this is just me guessing, the groaning noise could have come from the entity that scared the spirits away. This entity could have been a head nurse or disciplinarian. So maybe it was this entity that was groaning—its way of telling us to back off and leave them alone."

The background electromagnetic fields behaved erratically inside the old hospital building—odd indeed, considering that it was supposed to be completely devoid of power—and in the out-side grounds, particularly toward the end of their ghost hunt. Noel firmly believes that these EMF fluctuations were caused by the pres-ence of spirits, following the *Ghost Files Singapore* team around the old Changi Hospital out of pure curiosity. Curiously, Noel described a sense of great peacefulness and calm—no fear or anxiety was pres-ent whatsoever. He feels that the spirits of former patients or staff may have been clustering around the team, making good use of their last possibility to communicate with them before the boys left for the night.

Like any good paranormal research team, the crew from *Ghost Files Singapore* conducted some electronic voice phenomena (EVP) experiments during their visit to Changi. Although nothing was heard physically at the time of recording, when the audio files were played back from a session that was conducted inside the old nursery and children's ward, a small voice was heard saying the word "Papa."

"I think that voice was of a young girl," reflects Noel, when asked about the voice. "I still think about it till this day. It's stuff like this that really hits home. I have a soft spot for children and it always leaves me emotional. A huge part of me wishes they didn't die young. To know that children passed away and their spirits are still roaming the old Changi Hospital makes me sad. I believe in a heaven and I wish they were there instead. Just thinking about it now makes me upset."

Covering an area the size of an old hospital campus is diffi-cult at best, especially with a relatively small number of crew mem-bers available. The *Ghost Files Singapore* team helped to offset the few boots on the ground by placing some unmanned cameras and microphones upon the second floor. One can imagine their surprise when the recordings were played back, and the sound of not only a cough, but also an exhalation of some kind, were both recorded echoing through the empty corridors.

Could an intruder have perhaps snuck in and have been playing pranks upon them? Noel is adamant that this did not happen. "I can guarantee that nobody else was in area, yet alone the building."

Although the neighboring old commando barracks building has since been converted into a luxury hotel, the ruined shell of the old Changi Hospital still stands vacant and abandoned. There is talk of completely renovating the building that was once used for the care of children, with a view toward repurposing it for use as accommodation for students. Will the paranormal activity continue once the crumbling old building has been given a new face, but retain the same dark history? Noel Boyd has his own strongly-held opinions about what will happen then.

"I believe it will carry on unless they get mediums and priests to conduct blessings and cleansing," says Noel. "I highly doubt anyone would attempt to get rid of them. Instead they will try to appease these entities and attempt to get humans and entities to coexist with minimal disturbances. But there will be the mischievous ones that will scare humans from time to time."

Nowadays, security has been tightened around the complex. Motion sensors and alarms are employed to keep out the majority of paranormal thrill-seekers, leaving the skeleton of the old Changi Hospital to keep its secrets all to itself...and its ghosts.

CHAPTER 16

The Old Yoakum Memorial Hospital
Texas, USA

What started out as the Huth Memorial Hospital in 1922, with just an unlucky 13's worth of patient beds, eventually became the Yoakum Catholic Hospital by the early 1980s (several orders of nuns were instrumental in both staffing and expanding the facility from its humble early origins) and finally the Yoakum Community Hospital in 1988. Yoakum Community survived until 1997 when, like so many other small local community hospitals, it was supplanted by a bigger facility that was built in the area.

The hospital has stood abandoned and desolate ever since it officially closed its doors for the last time. A group of volunteers (and paranormal investigators) known as the old Yoakum Hospital Group now helps to protect and manage the facility, occasionally renting it out for the night to other interested teams of paranormal investigators who hope to uncover its ghostly secret. This is exactly how the Houston-based team of ghost hunters known as Contact Paranormal Research came to be there on a sunny spring morning in 2014.

When arriving at a supposedly haunted location for the first time, almost every good investigator likes to walk around the place in daylight, if possible. We're on the lookout for things like power lines, sources of running or standing water, and where the utilities enter the building—essentially, the lay of the land while we can still see without flashlights. Led by founder and lead investigator Jason Arnold, the team from Contact Paranormal arrived shortly before lunchtime and took advantage of a guided tour from a member of the Old Yoakum Hospital Group. They started off down in the basement. The volunteer then led them from one floor up to the next, walking through each one and pointing out areas of interest. No sooner had the group made it up to the second floor—which, according to both visiting ghost hunters and the volunteers of the Old Yoakum Hospital Group, is one of the most active paranormal hotspots in the hospital, if not *the* most active—when the crew was startled by a rather bizarre occurrence.

"As soon as we got to the second floor during the walk-through, we asked our tour guide, Lisa, a question about what is the most active floor," recounts Jason. "And she says, 'the second floor.' We asked about the ghost of the blue nun that is supposed to inhabit the second floor, and suddenly a patient door about 50 feet down the hallway slams shut. We checked each and every door on that same hallway, and none of them would close without giving them a good pull. There was no wind or drafts flowing up there, and no one was in the building except for us."

Paranormal investigators and staff members alike have a very good reason to suspect the second floor as being at the hub of the old hospital's ghostly activity. A 23-year-old female nursing student (who I have chosen not to name) was shot several times with a .22-caliber pistol while she was standing at the nursing station after an argument with her estranged husband. Although the cause of the quarrel remains unknown, we do know that it took place on that same floor, just outside the doors to the Intensive Care Unit.

Perhaps realizing the magnitude of what he had perpetrated, the panicked husband fled the scene of his crime, leaving the shocked doctors and nurses to carry his victim's body to a treatment bed inside the ICU, where they desperately tried to resuscitate her. Tragically, their efforts were to be in vain. Their colleague had already died of her wounds, one of which had unfortunately been inflicted to the head.

But what of her murderer? He was arrested by police officers at his mother's home without putting up a fight. The murder weapon was also recovered there. After being charged with murder and confined to jail awaiting his trial, the 24 year-old was subsequently sentenced to 99 years in prison. Now that the outcome was clear, he returned to his jail cell and tied a bed sheet to the frame of the shower cubicle. Drawing screams from the two other prisoners with whom he shared a cell, the now-convicted murdered hanged himself before their horrified eyes.

He did not deign to leave a suicide note.

The ghost of this poor, unfortunate nurse has been reported on numerous occasions to be seen walking through the hospital corridors, particularly in the second floor area surrounding the nurses station and the Intensive Care Unit where she was murdered. One hopes that this forlorn specter is a residual apparition—a "recording"–type ghost, much like the image on a TV screen—rather than an intelligent, earth-bound spirit.

With four floors of the haunted hospital to be covered, Jason and his team had their work cut out for them. Despite the fact that the team from Contact Paranormal strung out cabling that allowed them to connect up cameras and microphones on each one of those floors, nobody was surprised when the majority of the paranormal activity that night occurred up on the second floor. In addition to the ghost of the murdered nurse, the spirit of a young girl named Katie is supposed to haunt the second floor. Katie seems to be a mostly harmless, playful child spirit, hardly something to be afraid of. The male ghost said to inhabit the same floor, on the other hand, may be less than friendly. Contact Paranormal's host a member of the Old Yoakum Hospital Group, told them that this "shadow man" keeps Katie confined to specific areas within the hospital, not allowing her to roam freely throughout the building.

Psychics who have visited the old Yoakum Hospital say that the man is seen hovering over Katie, seeming to steer her in certain directions. When they ask him his name, he never replies to them. His identity remains a mystery. Katie, on the other hand, was more than willing to respond to those same psychics, confirming her name and the fact that she passed away while a patient in the hospital, but not what the cause of her death was. Katie's name has also been spoken on more than a few EVPs recorded at the hospital.

Whether this mysterious male spirit's intentions are protective or malevolent is a matter of some conjecture, but his existence is quite firmly established because it has been captured on camera. Members of the Old Yoakum Hospital Group consider their most impressive, convincing piece of evidence to be the apparition of a shadowy male figure, who was caught on an unmanned DVR camera, crossing from one side of a deserted corridor to the other. Quite a few people have reported seeing full body apparitions, they told me during an interview.

The shadow man is not restricted to the second floor, however. He has been seen on every floor of the hospital, and seems to enjoy roaming whenever and wherever the mood takes him. Another favorite spot is the area surrounding the elevator doorway on the first floor, where he has also been photographed.

As their overnight investigation transitioned from evening into the early hours of the morning, the old Yoakum Memorial Hospital gradually became more active; small things happened at first, such as unaccountable noises and sensations. But the phenomena soon grew to greater levels of impressiveness, such as the sound of footsteps heard ascending the empty staircase; when investigators went to check, nobody was found to account for the footsteps, and they had abruptly stopped.

The enigmatic shadow man seems to have put in a personal appearance himself, up on his familiar home turf, the second floor. Investigators Jason, Angela, and Melissa were staking out the second floor of the hospital, hanging out at the nurses' station close to the nursery. All appeared to be calm and quiet. Jason was the first to catch sight of a black figure, which darted from one side of the corridor to the other. As he opened his mouth to speak, the figure dashed back the way it had come. By the time the other investigators looked in that direction, the shadow man had disappeared.

Curious, the team went to check on the spot where the shadow man had been standing just seconds earlier. It was completely devoid of life, the corridor remaining still, silent, and gloomy. When the team checked their video footage and the digital photographs that they had taken, the shadow man was conspicuous by his absence, despite the team's best attempts to capture evidence of his presence.

But this was only the first of his many appearances that night. He seemed to be playing hide-and-go-seek with the team from Contact Paranormal, peering out at them from within the shadowy depths of the second-floor corridors, then ducking back out of sight again when he was spotted. Every time he was seen, the researchers went to investigate. Every time, they drew a blank. They estimate that this happened 10 times total over the course of their investigation. It was more than a little frustrating.

Not long afterward, Jason saw a dark figure rise up through the floor in one of the rooms just a few steps away from where the shadow man had been spotted. This figure also failed to appear in any of the recordings made by the team. It begins to look more and more like someone—or some*thing*—was stalking the team for its own amusement.

The second floor continued to be active throughout the night. As Angela, Melissa, and Cathy were investigating up there, a green light suddenly appeared at the far end of the corridor. The light floated down the hallway toward them, growing in size as it drew nearer. After it had travelled roughly 100 feet, the glowing ball made a sudden turn, disappearing through a set of double doors that separated the run-down old patient rooms from the former nursery.

In an attempt to entice the spirit of Katie to come out and make her presence known, two members of Contact Paranormal—Bill and Angela—hit upon the idea of playing a simple child's game. They settled upon rolling a ball back and forth between one another, hoping to coax the ghost of the young girl to come out and join in. Suddenly, a blast of air blew past them—something that should not be possible inside a closed-up building in the middle of the night, with no apparent source. One of the pre-positioned motion detectors was also triggered at the same time. Someone—or some*thing*— had moved through its infrared beam, disrupting it sufficiently to sound the alarm. Whatever it was that had done this, it did not appear on any of the camera recordings, and nothing was seen by the investigators.

A photograph taken that same night shows what the investigators at Contact Paranormal believe to be a pair of light anomalies, one positioned above the other, seemingly moving through an open doorway. It's tempting to dismiss images like this as simple "dust anomalies," which provides an explanation for a great many photographs that claim to show orbs and similar light anomalies. But it's worth pointing out that the CPR staff took more than a hundred photographs during their investigation of the old Yoakum Memorial Hospital and they threw out every single one that contained anything orb-like. Most surfaces inside this abandoned old building are covered in a fine coating of dust, which stirs up every time somebody moves past and disturbs the air currents, sending a cloud of dust particles into the air, which are just *begging* to reflect the light from a camera flash right back into the lens, thereby creating a smattering of orbs. This particular image is what remains once that type of picture has been tossed out, and whatever has been captured—whether it is paranormal or not—is too large and luminous to be explained away by dust particles.

One of the most intriguing things to happen all night took place inside the remains of the old operating theater. It was close to 6 a.m. on Sunday morning. The entire team was tired, fatigued from a very active night spent investigating the haunted old hospital. As the group of paranormal investigators was clustered together while conducting an EVP session, sitting on the dusty floor to take the weight off of their aching feet, Thomas happened to look up and catch sight of a human-shaped figure just behind Cathy's shoulder. The figure moved quickly past Cathy, who was unaware that the form was directly behind her, and passed through the doorway into Operating Theater Number Two.

Abandoning their EVP session for a moment, the group trouped into Operating Theater Number Two in pursuit of the figure. Despite searching it high and low, nothing out of the ordinary was to be found inside there. When it was suggested that they resume the EVP session once more and attempt to communicate with whatever the entity was that Thomas had observed, everybody settled down into a sitting position once more and began to record again.

Like all operating theaters, this was an interior room with no windows to the outside that would let the grey light of dawn seep in. It was completely dark and isolated in there, almost the ideal environment in which to record electronic voice phenomena.

Only a few minutes had passed before Cameron began to notice something very unusual: a mist was forming, seemingly out of thin air. When ghost hunters encounter inexplicable mists during the course of their investigations, they tend to be a shade of grey, black, or white in color. The mist seen by the team from Contact Paranormal was described as being a sort of pinkish hue, and was subsequently seen by all five of them. It appeared to originate at the level of the ceiling, slowly coalescing there before creeping down one wall toward the floor, where it then faded away before the incredulous eyes of Jason Arnold and his crew.

All of this took less than a minute. In the cold light of day, it's easy to ask why none of those gathered in the room immediately snatched up a camera and started shooting video footage or snapping still photos. "We were in total awe the entire time," Jason explained to me in an email. "Nobody *thought* to pick up a camera or a recorder."

This phenomenon is one that occurs over and over again among paranormal investigators. "I was so taken aback, it never even crossed my mind to grab my camera!" is something that I have heard again and again over the years. It does not matter how motivated and professional a researcher you are—until the day comes when you finally come face to face with something that is truly and inarguably paranormal, you never know how you will react. All bets are off.

Jason and his team are far from the only investigators to make contact with the ghosts of the old Yoakum Memorial Hospital, as it formed another stopping-off point for ghost-hunting DJ Russell Rush on his *Haunted Tour*. When interviewing his contact from the Old Yoakum Hospital Group[1], Russell learned about the hospital's former resident chaplain, Father Kraum. Struck down by polio as a youth, this man of great religious faith might have been wheelchair-bound, but he wasn't about to let that stop him from preaching and spreading the word of God. The Father gave mass on a very regular basis, and became something of a fixture at the hospital, much loved by both staff and patients alike. In fact, his wheelchair can still be seen there to this day, kept reverently parked inside the chapel where he spent so many happy hours sermonizing and connecting spiritually with his flock.

Although Father Kraum's apparition has not been reported (so far as we know) the chapel *is* a paranormal hotspot, particularly when it comes to the capture of EVPs and other auditory phenomena. When asked about the chapel, the long-term volunteer custodians of the hospital say that they are not 100 percent sure of the identity of the chapel's ghost—only that it *is* haunted by an entity of some kind. As to who that might be—they prefer to hedge their bets.

Paranormal investigator Hazel Bishop and her colleagues experienced the sound of running footsteps when they investigated Yoakum, and also caught the sound of a whistle on the otherwise empty first floor. "Due to the amount of personal experiences we have had at this location, we would recommend it to anyone who wants to investigate," says Hazel. She considers the chapel to be one of the most paranormally active parts of the building, particularly as her team received disembodied knocks in answer to questions that they asked while investigating in there.

What does it *feel* like to walk the corridors of this extremely haunted former hospital? "The first floor is particularly creepy, probably due to the lack of lighting and electricity," a long-time volunteer told me during an interview. "The north end is always very cold and drafty. The second floor feels a little more normal, due to there being some lights and power still running there." Investigators tend to avoid the third floor, as the roof has been in a poor state of repair. Years of leaking has resulted in mold growing up there.

But the feel of the building changes, dependent upon the personalities present at the time. "I've been in there so many times over the years," the volunteer told me. "Sometimes the building feels normal. But on others, it just doesn't feel...*right*. And those are the nights when the old hospital turns out to be very active."

The Old Yoakum Hospital is still available for rental to responsible paranormal research groups. If you happen to live within traveling distance, why not head along and see for yourself whether you can encounter the enigmatic shadow man, or one of the multitude of other restless spirits who reside within its walls?

It is only fitting that I leave the final words to those good people who continue to voluntarily devote their time and expertise to one of the hospital's "guardian angels," the men and women of the Old Yoakum Hospital Group:

> Of course we are trying to establish that the building is haunted and we feel that it is sometimes more than others times. We really enjoyed having this opportunity to experiment in the paranormal and offer it to others to experience what they can get to, however, the hospital will not be here forever so we're trying to get as much done as possible before it eventually ends. This hospital has a great history and is a time-honored tradition in this community and we honor and respect everything that it has done for the community and for the spirits that may personally live there still.

St. Albans Sanatorium
Radford, Virginia, USA

Originally a prep school for boys during the 19th century, run by a Professor named George Miles, this 68,000-foot building was intended to help young men get a good start in life before going on to a university education. It changed roles significantly in the early 1900s and became a specialized hospital for taking care of those afflicted with mental illness. It remained an active sanatorium until the 1980s, when it closed its doors as a healthcare institution and subsequently passed into private hands. Unlike some of the other asylums that we have encountered throughout this book, the patient care delivered at St. Albans had a reputation for being relatively humane.

It was far from perfect, however. The field of mental health care had a long way to go (and indeed, still does) and patients sometimes died when subjected to some of the more radical therapies of the time, such as insulin therapy, in which the patient's blood sugar was dropped to dangerously low levels due to the repeated administration of high-dose insulin. This would slam the patient into a comatose state, from which they would gradually re-awaken (unless, of course, they died) and then the "therapy" would be repeated. It was a particularly common treatment for those who had been diagnosed with schizophrenia.

In the pantheon of modern medicine, insulin therapy deserves a place somewhere close to using leeches to suck the blood. There was never any convincing rationale for using it, and yet British and American hospitals were employing it as recently as the 1970s.

The human brain is an extremely irritable organ. Deprive it of sugar for any great length of time, and the brain will express its displeasure by causing a seizure. During the seizure, the patient stands a chance of not only vomiting, but also inhaling that vomit down into the lungs, running the risk of dying through a condition known as "aspiration pneumonia." Dying was not the worst thing that could happen to a patient who was subjected to such a treatment. If revived with glucose injections before death occurred, the brain may already have been irreversibly damaged, and the unfortunate patient placed into a horrific vegetative state from which they might never recover.

Several different types of "shock therapies" would have been practiced as St. Albans. Despite them being administered by caring medical professionals in what they believed to be the best interests of their patients, the procedures would most definitely have killed people. Additionally, there are a number of documented suicides within the building. One of the bathrooms, in which four patients supposedly killed themselves, has been nicknamed "the suicide room" by those who take care of St. Albans today.

"When the current owners bought the place six years ago, they found a historical note on the wall of this particular bathroom," explained head of security, Chuck Thornton. "We're not sure who left it. But the note was telling the story of a member of staff who was in that same bathroom many years ago, cleaning it. The cleaner heard a voice say, 'you'd better scrub and scrub, because there's no amount of scrubbing that will remove the blood that's been spilled in this room.' They dropped their cleaning equipment and fled!"

The suicide bathroom is far from the only haunted area of St. Albans. Ghostly children are seen throughout the building, usually the ghosts of little girls. Down in the basement is the former bowling alley, the walls now covered with graffiti. Displaying a fine sense of humor, the resident spirit is a young girl who has been nicknamed "Allie." A white misty cloud has been witnessed drifting through the bowling alley, disappearing before the eyes of those who saw it. Still others reported encountering a malevolent entity down in the basement, which is referred to as "Red Eyes."

In keeping with the theme of appropriate nicknames, the "Rocker Room" is so-called because it is home to a rocking chair, which has been seen to rock backward and forward, as though being pushed by some unseen occupant. Or what about the "Whistle Room," in which you might whistle one of your favorite tunes—and receive a shrill response from the unidentified spirit that resides there.

St. Albans may also be the last resting place of a murder victim. Eight days after her disappearance, 18-year-old Gina Renee Hall's car was discovered on June 28, 1980. The vehicle—still stained with the unfortunate victim's blood—was found on a street not far from the sanatorium. She was last seen at a dance club in nearby Blacksburg, and then believed to have gone to a lakeside cabin with her killer. Bloodstains of a type that matched Gina's were discovered at the cabin, but her body was nowhere to be found. It is believed that a man named Stephen Epperly made sexual overtures to Gina, and that when she rejected him, he killed her in a fit of rage.

One unique aspect of this tragic case is that the killer is the first person ever to be convicted of murder in the state of Virginia without a body ever being recovered. Epperly is currently serving a life sentence in jail, and maintained at trial that he was innocent. But rumors circulated at the time of the murder that Gina's body may have been secreted in freshly poured concrete on the grounds of St. Albans—perhaps because it was commonly believed that Epperly may have been briefly employed at the sanatorium.

In an attempt to answer this question, medium Amy Allan and former homicide detective Steve Di Schiavi conducted an investigation at St. Albans for the fifth season of their show *The Dead Files*. The premise of the show is simple: What commonalities will a psychic medium and a trained cop come up with, independently of one another, when they investigate a haunted location?

Amy said that she was picking up on the ghosts of four women who she thought wanted to leave the sanatorium, but could not. She reported experiencing a woman running up to her and screaming at her, which coincides with the scream heard by the owner, a lady named Marcelle, who felt that she had startled one of the resident spirits. A number of emaciated spirits were hammering at the windows and wailing, trying to escape.

She also picked up on the presence of a tall male spirit who was acting as a protector for the others there, setting up a kind of "spiritual safe zone." He wanted Amy to leave, and if she would not, threatened to hurt her. Although this spirit was young in appearance, she believed that he was older and deliberately projecting a younger appearance.

Professor George Miles, the driving force behind the St. Albans School for Boys, died of liver cancer at the age of 42. According to a local historian, although some people believed that George Miles was a good man, others thought that he was not quite the savory character that he first appeared. Could he perhaps be the male spirit "projecting a younger appearance" and acting as a kind of jailer for other entities within St. Albans? The answer remains unclear, although Marcelle, responsible for overseeing St. Albans, does not believe so.

Interviewing Chuck Thornton, Steve Di Schiavi learned that there was one room in particular where female visitors had been inappropriately touched: the boiler room. The problem had gotten so bad that women were no longer allowed in that room alone.

On her walkthrough, Amy mentioned picking up on what she described as a "pervy" male spirit, who liked to touch the hair of women in that room—and she suspected that the touching did not stop at just their hair. And if you think that things could not possibly get any creepier, the spirit wanted her to address him as "uncle."

Without knowledge of the murder, Amy picked up on a man being teased in that area by a young woman, who would not allow him to kiss her. The young man then hit her, and Amy went on to say that she believed a rape occurred after the physical attack.

Tempting as it may be to conclude that the physical assault and possible sexual assault of Gina Hall was being picked up on, prosecutors believed that she was murdered at Claytor Lake, not within the confines of St. Albans. One key piece of information missing from this episode of *The Dead Files* is the era of clothing worn by these two ghostly figures—1980s, or older?

Several people appear to have been overcome by whatever forces reside within the walls of St. Albans. In my interview with him, Chuck Thornton related multiple instances of visitors to the sanatorium (usually paranormal investigators) who began to speak in bizarre tongues, and in some terrifying instances their eyes would turn an opaque black color. "The only way we could get 'em back to normal was to pray over them," he told me matter-of-factly.

This tracks with what was experienced by psychic Amy Allan, who felt that the spirit of a woman entered into her body at St. Albans and refused to leave it when asked. She was partially "taken over" by this entity, something that is extremely rare for the experienced psychic medium. It took eight hours for her to cleanse the invading spirit from her body afterward. The spirit told Amy that there were a lot of dead people who could do what she did, and were capable of provoking some living human beings toward self-harm or suicide.

Chuck Thornton has also undergone the unnerving experience of being gripped by something unseen but powerful, levitated up from one of the steps on the staircase, and then thrown toward a nearby doorway. Chuck is a former law enforcement officer, and is therefore a trained observer of events—and in my book, a very credible witness.

When leaving the gift shop one day and climbing the steps, he could see something "with rippling chest muscles" as he climbed the stairs, which picked him up in an immensely strong bear-hug.

Not all of the spirits that haunt St. Albans are as unfriendly as this alpha male, however. Chuck has frequently encountered the apparitions of two women, somewhere between their mid-20s and early 30s, often accompanied by the spirit of a little girl around 7 or 8 years old. They all wear late-19th century period white dresses, and like to follow him around the place as he makes his rounds.

At the time of writing (the summer of 2015), St. Albans is as paranormally active as ever, if not more so. "Just last night," Chuck told me during our interview, "we had a team of ghost hunters investigating the suicide bathroom. They were using a spirit box, and they kept hearing from this foul-mouthed entity that was swearing at them, using real nasty language.

"It kept trying to get one of them to lay down in the bathtub. Now they wouldn't do it, but if they had . . . I just know that one of them would have been taken over. They would have been *possessed*."

NOTES

Chapter 2

1. "Abandoned to the vandals, the Grade II-listed former military hospital that treated generations of servicemen," *Daily Mail,* 1 April 2012.
2. "Ghost turns up on Grantham urban explorer's photo," *Grantham Journal,* September 16 2013.

Chapter 3

1. "The Halloween Haunts Scream Park: An all-local Hallow's Eve haunt," *The Manila Times,* October 30 2013.
2. " 'Ghost tourism' drawing visitors to former U.S. base," *The Philippine Star,* October 31 2012.

Chapter 4

1. Katherine A. Kean. "State Hospital story began on a note of hope," *Times Record/Roane County Reporter,* July 6, 1989.
2. George Dudding. *Inside Haunted Spencer State Hospital.* GSD Publications, 2014.

Chapter 5

1. Victoria public records pertaining to Agency VA 2841.
2. Ararat (Asylum 1867–1905; Hospital for the Insane 1905–1934; Mental Hospital 1934-ct).
3. *http://en.wikipedia.org/wiki/J_Ward.*

4. Ararat J-Ward Investigation Report, Ghost Research International, 2007.

5. *www.jward.org.au/faqs.html.*

Chapter 6

1. You can listen to the EVPs recorded by Paranormal EXP over at their website, *www.paranormalexp.com/linda-vista-community-hospital-boyle-heights-cas/.*

2. Roger Vincent. "Historic L.A. hospital site to be turned into senior apartments," *L.A. Times,* May 16, 2012.

3. Esmerelda Bermudez. "Some disquiet on these L.A. film sets," *L.A. Times,* April 4, 2010.

4. Ibid.

5. Nick Groff and Jeff Belanger. *Chasing Spirits—The Building of the Ghost Adventures Crew.* New York: New American Library, 2012.

Chapter 7

1. Elliot. O'Donnell. *Haunted Waters.* The Anchor Press, 1957.

2. Peter Underwood. *Haunted London.* Amberley Publishing, 2010.

Chapter 8

1. *www.robinsaikia.com/p/poveglia-island-of-sadness-and-terror.html.*

Chapter 10

1. *www.ucl.ac.uk/Bentham-Project/who/autoicon/Virtual_Auto_Icon.*

2. Peter Underwood. *Haunted London.* Amberley Publishing, 2010.

Chapter 11

1. *www.therussellrushhauntedtour.com/articles/2012-investigations-464710/yorktown-memorial-hospital-10511381.*

2. "Group set to capitalize on apparitions at Yorktown Hospital," *San Antonio Current,* September 27, 2011.

3. *Ghost Adventures: Aftershocks,* season one, episode six.

4. "A night at Yorktown Memorial Hospital," *Victoria Advocate,* April 2, 2011.

5. You can listen to the audio file of the squeaking cart, along with the rest of Contact Paranormal's EVP evidence, over at

www.contactparanormalresearch.com/investigation-of-yorktown-memorial-hospital.html.

Chapter 12
1. You can enjoy the Danvers adventure of Brian and the *SCARED!* crew at *www.youtube.com/watch?v=HkQAPVJ-RrI&feature=youtu.be.*
2. Ibid.

Chapter 13
1. *http://psican.org/alpha/index.php?/Alberta-Ghost-Reports/Grace-Hospital.html.*
2. "New private facility woos public dollars in Calgary," *Canadian Medical Association Journal* 159 (1998): 551–552.

Chapter 14
1. *www.youtube.com/watch?v=Z6gyTX2bNCg.*
2. "Mental patient held in dismemberment murder," *St Joseph, Missouri, Gazette*, August 13, 1980.
3. *www.youtube.com/watch?v=kw8t1S0KGs4.*
4. *http://creepychusetts.blogspot.com/2010/10/metfern-cemetery-waltham-2-2.html.*
5. *www.oddthingsiveseen.com/2013/09/abandoned-accessible-and-awesome.html.*

Chapter 15
1. *http://remembersingapore.org/old-changi-hospital/.*
2. *www.hungzai.com/changi-hospital-trip/.*
3. *www.hungzai.com/visit-to-och/.*
4. *www.hungzai.com/went-to-changi-hospital/.*
5. *www.hungzai.com/tales-of-old-changi-hospital/.*
6. *www.hungzai.com/old-changi-hospital-2/.*

Chapter 16
1. You can watch this interview, and more from Russell's investigation, here: *www.therussellrushhauntedtour.com/articles/2014-investigations-489252/old-yoakum-community-hospital-12906199/.*

INDEX

ABOUT THE AUTHOR

Richard Estep was born and raised in Leicester, England. After several years investigating the paranormal in the United Kingdom, Richard brought his lifelong passion for all things ghostly along with him when he relocated to the United States in 1999, where he continues to investigate cases of hauntings on both sides of the Atlantic.

Although Richard earns his living as a paramedic, clinical educator, and assistant chief for a private ambulance company, he also volunteers as a firefighter, teaches new EMTs and paramedics at several EMS academies, and serves on Colorado's federal Disaster Medical Assistance Team (DMAT) #3. When he isn't creeping around old buildings looking for ghosts, he likes to unwind by reading, playing tabletop and video games, and constructing a ridiculous amount of Legos.

Richard is married to Laura, and together they have been adopted by five rescue cats and a dog (please don't tell their homeowner's association). Richard is also the author of *In Search of the Paranormal* and *Haunted Longmont*.